HEROES OF NEW YORK HARBOR
TALES FROM THE CITY'S PORT

MARIAN BETANCOURT

Foreword by
Captain Brian McAllister and Edmond Moran Jr.

Globe
Pequot

Guilford, Connecticut

Globe
Pequot

An imprint of Rowman & Littlefield

Distributed by NATIONAL BOOK NETWORK

Copyright © 2017 by Marian Betancourt

Map: Alena J. Pearce © Rowman & Littlefield

British Library Cataloguing in Publication Information Available

Library of Congress Cataloging-in-Publication Data Available

ISBN 978-1-4930-2430-8 (paperback)
ISBN 978-1-4930-2431-5 (e-book)

∞™ The paper used in this publication meets the minimum requirements of American National Standard for Information Sciences—Permanence of Paper for Printed Library Materials, ANSI/ NISO Z39.48-1992.

So the crowd moved on and on, while the great harbor, surrounding their lives and shaping their lives, went on with its changes unheeded.
ERNEST POOLE, *THE HARBOR*, 1915

This is for my late father, Beauregard Charles Betancourt, who may not have been aware of it at the time, but he did pass along his love of the harbor.

Also for Captain Christian Martin Petersen, the great grandfather I wish I had known.

And as always, this is for my son, Tom, and my daughter, Karen.

Contents

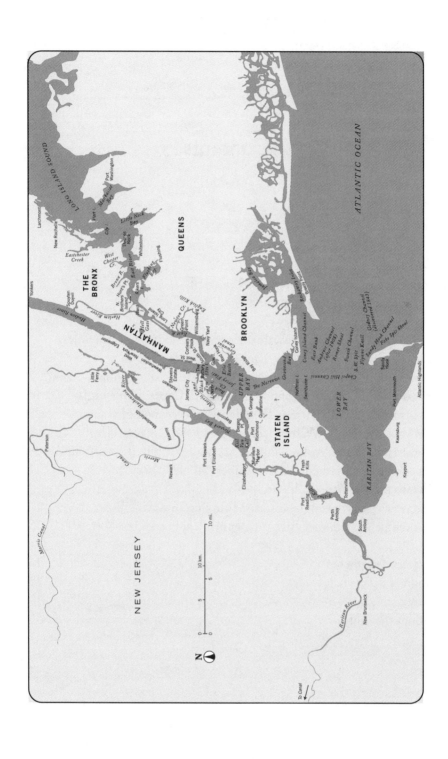

N

NEW JERSEY

Paterson

Morris Canal

Hackensack River

Little Ferry

Meadowlands

Kearny

Newark

Passaic River

Merris Canal

Port Elizabeth

Port Newark

Elizabethport

Mariners Harbor

Port Reading

Port Amboy

South Amboy

Raritan River

New Brunswick

To Canal

STATEN ISLAND

Arthur Kill

Fresh Kills

Totterville

Kill Van Kull

Port Richmond

Bergen Pt.

St. George

Quarantine

Bayonne

Newark Bay

Jersey City

Hoboken

Stevens Estate

Weehawken

West New York

Edgewater

Hudson River

MANHATTAN

Spuyten Duyvil

Yonkers

Harlem River

Hell Gate

Long Island City

Astoria

Bowery Bay

Riker's I.

North Brother I.

Brothers I.

Hunt's Pt.

Bronx R.

East River

Flushing

Little Neck Bay

Whitestone

College Pt.

Throgs Neck

City I.

West Chester Cr.

Eastchester Creek

New Rochelle

Larchmont

Port Washington

Manhasset Bay

Hart I.

LONG ISLAND SOUND

THE BRONX

QUEENS

BROOKLYN

Jamaica Bay

Rockaway Inlet

Breezy Point

Coney Island

Corey Island

East Bank

Ambrose Channel (after 1908)

Romer Shoal

Swash Channel

Chapel Hill Channel

S.W. Spit

Flynns Knoll

Gedney's Channel (abandoned 1865)

Sandy Hook Channel

False Hook Channel

Sandy Hook

LOWER BAY

RARITAN BAY

Keansburg

Port Monmouth

Keyport

Atlantic Highlands

ATLANTIC OCEAN

UPPER BAY

The Narrows

Governors I.

Hoffman I.

Swinburne I.

Bay Ridge

Gowanus Canal

Red Hook

Navy Yard

Williamsburg

Newtown Creek

Buttermilk C.

Governors I.

Bedloe's I.

Ellis I.

Erie Basin

Corlears Hook

Wallabout

Blackwell's I.

Black Tom

Morris C.

Communipaw

Greenpoint

West St.

Hurl Gate

Brother Is.

Corlears Hook

10 mi.

10 km.

0   5   10

Foreword

THIS BOOK TELLS THE STORY OF NEW YORK HARBOR THROUGH ITS PEO-
ple, those who made a difference helping it become the great port it was
and is today. Our company names are well known because of the tugboats
still working here after more than a century and a half when our families
established them, but few other names immediately come to mind, even
to native New Yorkers. Many terrific books have been written about the
harbor, but few tell the human story.

It's unlikely that the visitors who enter Castle Clinton at the Battery
to buy tickets to the Statue of Liberty ferry know that it was originally a
fort planned and built by Jonathan Williams, grandnephew of Benjamin
Franklin, who also created the fort on Governors Island to protect us
from the British as the War of 1812 was heating up. It worked because
the British decided to attack Washington, DC, instead. The Williamsburg neighborhood along the East River is named for this engineer who
was also the first superintendent of West Point.

A narrow passage of erratic currents, aptly named Hell Gate, leads
the East River out into the Long Island Sound, the so-called back door
to the harbor. It was like a turnstile for ships, filled with boulders, reefs,
whirlpools, and other obstacles that caused so many shipwrecks that most
sailors would not venture through the passage without a good supply of
whisky to fortify their nerves. It wasn't until Civil War veteran Lt. Colonel John Newton of the Army Corps of Engineers took on the task that
it was cleared. The largest and final obstacle, Flood Rock, was destroyed
in 1885 with six times the greatest explosive charge ever fired in the

world until the atomic bomb. This was so carefully planned and Newton so confident that he allowed his adored little daughter to pull the switch. Thousands of spectators lining the shores felt hardly a tremor.

In the early days our tugboats were often leased by the newspapers not only to report on what ships were arriving or leaving and who was on them, but what sorts of mischief might be afloat in the harbor. For example, reporters avidly followed the activities of Dynamite Johnny O'Brien, who literally grew up in the harbor and probably knew it better than anyone. This cocky and diminutive man was already famous among sailors for his extraordinary skill as a pilot guiding windjammers through the treacherous currents of Hell Gate before it was cleared out, but when he outmaneuvered Spanish gunboats and United States revenue cutters to keep the Cuban rebels supplied with weapons and recruits in the 1890s, he became a legend.

The name Roebling is well known, but you may not realize that it was Emily Roebling who carried on the work of the chief engineer for the last fourteen years of the construction of the Brooklyn Bridge. Her husband, Washington Roebling, was incapacitated and nearly blind from caisson's disease (also known as decompression sickness, or the bends), which he acquired early on at the site. Emily was well educated and well versed in engineering. She was respected by the bridge workers, but never got the credit she deserved because back then it was not considered suitable or even believable that a woman could take on such a task.

Katherine Walker, known as Lighthouse Kate, operated the Robbins Reef Light on a hidden ridge of submerged rocks at the mouth of the Kill Van Kull between Staten Island and Bayonne, New Jersey, that once caused numerous shipwrecks. From 1886 to 1919, Kate, barely five feet tall and weighing less than one hundred pounds, rescued as many as fifty people by her own count, and at least one dog. And while her two children were young, each weekday Kate rowed them a mile to and from school on Staten Island.

Ambrose Channel was created at the turn of the last century to allow the increasingly larger ships to enter the harbor through the Narrows. John Wolfe Ambrose, an Irish immigrant, might today be considered a Renaissance man because of his many interests and talents. He worked his way through New York University and Princeton, built the Second Avenue elevated subway, designed the city's street cleaning program, started a ferry to south Brooklyn, and built an amusement park there that saw the likes of Buffalo Bill and Annie Oakley. But his tireless decade-long effort to convince Congress to appropriate funds to deepen the shipping channel through the Narrows that made New York a world port is his most lasting gift.

Irving T. Bush, who inherited wealth and didn't have to work at all, had an idea to build a manufacturing complex on the waterfront where goods could be produced, stored, and shipped from the same location via water and rail to all parts of the world. Nobody believed it would work, and the project, begun at the end of the nineteenth century, was soon termed Bush's Folly. It worked beautifully, however, and Bush Terminal was the first of its kind, the largest multi-tenant industrial park in the nation.

In 1937 a trucker named Malcolm McLean hauled a load of cotton bales up from North Carolina to Hoboken where he had to wait an entire day before his truck was unloaded. He thought it ridiculous to spend so much time waiting. Why couldn't he just put his truck right on the ship, maybe take the wheels off and put them back on at the other end? The rest, as they say is history, but it took McLean twenty years to convince less enlightened shippers and New York harbor bosses of the idea's merits. While others may have had similar ideas, it was McLean who made it work. In 1956 his first container ship, the *Ideal X*, left New York harbor and by 1962 the Port of New York and New Jersey was the world's first container port. McLean, who died here at 87 in 2001, changed the nature of shipping and the harbor forever.

On September 11, 2001, US Coast Guard admiral Richard Bennis organized a waterborne escape for half a million people who flocked to the waterfront to get away from the devastation of the fallen towers when all other avenues of escape were closed. Bennis had been headed south to rest and recover from surgery when he heard the news and turned back to take charge of his command. As Captain of the Port, Bennis, with only a cell phone at his disposal, organized a flotilla of more than 100 boats that ran day and night, not only for the evacuation but to bring in crews and supplies. We were all there, tugs, excursion boats, ferries, yachts, Fire and Police Department boats. Admiral Bennis led the Coast Guard in strengthening its harbor presence from one of response to prevention as it left its auspices with the Treasury Department to become part of the new Department of Homeland Security. Admiral Craig Bone, who followed Bennis as Captain of the Port, extended that protection, as the Guard added more sophisticated surveillance systems that allow detection of suspicious activity many miles out to sea.

You will get to know these heroes as well as some of our own ancestors who, in the middle of the nineteenth century, were known collectively as the Irish Navy. New York had become the largest Irish city in the world and many in this population found their calling in the harbor's water traffic of windjammers, steamboats, barges, lighters, tugs, and hundreds of ferries that crisscrossed the harbor before we had bridges and tunnels. The great grandfather of this book's author piloted several of those ferries, and we won't hold it against him that he was Norwegian rather than Irish.

Our families were also called upon to provide vital services to our nation during wartime. During World War I Captain Jim McAllister sat on the Board of Embarkation and served as acting director for the Army's floating equipment, transporting explosives and troops through New York harbor, avoiding the danger posed by German U-boats lurking outside the port. In World War II Edmond Moran, considered a preeminent expert in tugboat operations, helped the American and British navies organize the fleet of tugs needed to tow massive concrete artificial harbors across the English Channel to support the D-Day invasion.

Today our harbor is much different from when our great grandfathers came here. Airlines have replaced passenger liners for long-distance travel and container ships replaced freighters, drastically reducing the number of ships needed to transport cargo. There are fewer tugs today too, from a high of eight hundred in 1929 to fewer than two hundred, but they are stronger and more environmentally friendly. Some of the piers that once lined the shore of the entire 1,500 square miles of waterfront are finding new purpose, such as the Chelsea Piers, now a recreational site on Manhattan's west Side.

The Port of New York and New Jersey is one of the most important and beautiful harbors in the world. Our tugs are working in many other cities, but New York is still home. McAllister and Moran have outlasted many other towing companies, and while we are still arch competitors, the two of us have always been personal friends.

Captain Brian McAllister, Chairman, McAllister Towing

Edmond (Ned) Moran Jr., Senior Vice President, Moran Towing Corporation

Introduction

The Bay Ridge Anchorage:
An Ever-Changing Canvas

BEFORE I TURN IN EACH NIGHT, I WAVE GOODNIGHT TO Ms. LIBERTY, who faces Brooklyn and my sixth floor window. She is my anchor and all is well in the world, or at least in my harbor. In the morning I approach my window with anticipation of the new colors and shapes on the ever-changing canvas that is the Bay Ridge Anchorage. Here, along the south Brooklyn shore, container ships, tankers and barges park while waiting to reload and be on their way around the world. A long black tanker is topped with a layered white wheelhouse. A bright orange cargo ship with a pink hull and white cabin supports deck cranes sitting like giant grasshoppers.

These colorful ship shapes arrange themselves on my canvas as if Matisse had come in the night and moved his paper cutouts around. All else pales next to this spectacular palette, even the bright green spring leaves and lawns growing along the shore. I recall one dark afternoon when lightning danced across the water like a point guard racing for the basket before the final bell. At twilight pinks and lavenders streak the sky and at sunset, the colors blaze into shocking pinks and gold as if announcing the call to cocktail hour. Two little red tugs, one aft and one astern, push and pull a big brown container barge into place before darkness descends.

This nautical parking lot is adjacent to the tidal strait between Brooklyn and Staten Island known as the Narrows, the cinched waist of land curves connected by the Verrazano Bridge. The orange Staten Island Ferries on which I spent many years, and about which my father wrote a small book, traverse the harbor, passing each other in front of Ms. Liberty through the day and night. The high-speed hydrofoil commuter ferry between Wall Street and Atlantic Highlands, New Jersey, on which my daughter sometimes commutes, churns up a trail of white froth as it comes through. Cruise ships glide regally by late Saturday afternoons, like big wedding cakes.

Stationary images frame this changing canvas. On my top left is the white fan-shaped structure around the Staten Island Ferry terminal; the pale granite buildings of Jersey City are a distant Stonehenge to the top right. Directly across from me gantry cranes at the Newark container ship port stick up like giant check marks on the horizon, reminding me of how much the harbor has changed in my lifetime. My far right anchor, at the tip of Manhattan, is the new World Trade Center, higher and more glittering than its predecessor, whose death I witnessed from this window.

I write from a desk in front of this moving tableau and occasionally, I am so enthralled that I dash off a descriptive phrase in an e-mail to a friend or colleague. It seems ironic now, but my first day job long ago, while attending college at night, also involved a desk by the window facing the water. Then, however, it was from Pier 3 North River, in the United Fruit Company offices. I spent much time looking away from my typewriter and out the window, watching ships go by and wondering when I would get a chance to go with one of them. That particular harborscape no longer exists, however, as landfill to create Battery Park City and the first World Trade Center replaced the old piers and the break bulk freighters and passenger liners have found other purposes. Then, as a newspaper reporter in the early 1970s, I chronicled the death of Brooklyn's Columbia Street waterfront, once a thriving neighborhood of longshoremen and their families, as containerization dramatically changed their lives and the harbor.

It took a discovery in Paris, however, to focus my attention on just how much the harbor means to me. A couple of decades ago, while browsing in Shakespeare and Company, the famous Left Bank bookstore, I came across a copy of *The Harbor*, a novel by Ernest Poole published in 1915. *The Harbor*, which spent several months on the *New York Times* best-seller list, is the story of New York as the change from sail to steam was remaking the harbor, and the effect it had on the lives of those who worked here. An idealistic boy, very much like Poole himself, tries to mitigate the cruelties of poverty and joblessness to find a solution to the woes of the people he had grown up with. (With his next book, Poole would become the first winner of the Pulitzer Prize. *The Harbor* was reissued by Penguin Classics in 2011.)

I strongly identified with Poole's book, which I have read several times, because during that time my own family history was beginning in the harbor. My great-grandfather was a ferry pilot before the bridges and tunnels were built, a time when there were so many boats in the harbor that traffic jams and collisions were not uncommon. Christian Martin Petersen left his home on the southern coast of Norway at thirteen. After sojourns with the Dutch and British navies, he came to New York in 1874 to work as first mate on the big yachts of James Gordon Bennett Jr., the *Dauntless* and the *Henrietta*. Then, as the family grew, he took a steadier job piloting ferryboats. As a child my dad often skipped school and with his younger brothers rode the ferry back and forth with his grandfather.

Just as in Earnest Poole's lifetime, the harbor has changed dramatically in my lifetime, too. When I was born, the port of New York was the busiest in the world and the center of heightened security during World War II. My dad loved photographing ships and he filled many scrapbooks with his photos along with articles he clipped from magazines and newspapers and eventually wrote his own small book about the Staten Island Ferry. While my relationship with my father was estranged because of divorce, it was the love of the harbor that eventually bound us together. When he picked me up from my Brooklyn home to stay with him for a weekend, we rode the Staten Island Ferry. His interest was in the boats and ships—and taking me on tours of engine rooms in which I had no interest. I wanted to know about the people who worked in the harbor and like most people, I especially loved the tugboats.

I found the Morans and McAllisters and first wrote about them in articles for *Irish America* magazine. And while investigating these tugboat families, I discovered the notorious harbor pilot Dynamite Johnny O'Brien. Looking into his adventures and visiting his grave on City Island with one of his great-granddaughters was a memorable experience. More recently I returned to the gravesite to meet with the Irish film crew chronicling O'Brien's role in aiding the Cuban rebels before the Spanish-American War.

I'm sure my great-grandfather knew of Dynamite Johnny O'Brien and the McAllister and Moran tugboat families, and the others of his day. When I learned that one of Michael Moran's early tug pilots liked to sing "Rock of Ages" at the top of his lungs while piloting his tug, it reminded me that my great-grandfather, according to my dad, also loved to sing while on the water.

I had the good fortune to live in a high-rise in Brooklyn Heights during the centennial celebrations of the Brooklyn Bridge and the Statue of Liberty, which reminded me of many of the people in this book who experienced the opening day celebrations, while the Great Bridge (1883) and Ms. Liberty (1886) were taking their places as American icons for all time. One of my favorite places to take a walk is over the Brooklyn Bridge.

Long ago, before I "rediscovered" my harbor, I often dreamed of escape to some other place, yearned to "put down roots" in a pretty house with lots of land. It took several failed attempts to leave before I realized my roots are here in this great harbor. And they are very deep.

I look forward to a new harbor tableau each morning and it really pleases me that all of the action has relocated to my end of the harbor.

Jonathan Williams:
Keeping Us Safe from Enemies

Engineers do not deal in magic; there must be sufficiency of time, money, with a very good stock of patience, or their works will never do any good to the public nor credit to themselves. If this harbor and bay were in possession of any one of the belligerent powers of Europe, their engineers would pronounce it to be perfectly defensible, but they would require a good fund of the three requisites before mentioned, money, time, and patience.
—JONATHAN WILLIAMS, AUGUST 17, 1807

IT'S UNLIKELY THAT MANY RESIDENTS OF THE WILLIAMSBURG SECTION of Brooklyn know that their neighborhood along the East River is named for Jonathan Williams, a civil engineer, scientist, philosopher, and grandnephew of Benjamin Franklin. In 1802, he was hired by Richard Woodhull, the operator of a ferry from the foot of today's Metropolitan Avenue, to lay out building lots and streets. Woodhull was apparently so pleased with the work that he named the settlement for the engineer.

Williams's most lasting contribution to New York, however, was the design and construction of the inner forts in the harbor, including Castle Williams on Governors Island and what is now Castle Clinton at the Battery. Once the British cleared out on November 25, 1783, forever after known as "Evacuation Day," New York harbor quickly became an economic powerhouse for the new nation, with shipping to and from Europe and other parts of the globe accounting for one-third of its income.

But it was defenseless.

ONE OF THE WORLD'S GREAT NATURAL HARBORS

Along with San Francisco, Halifax, Hamburg, and Sydney, New York's harbor is considered one of the ten best natural harbors in the world. Such harbors are protected by land, have calmer waves, are deep enough for anchorage, and don't require the construction of artificial breakwaters. They also have great naval and strategic importance. Centuries ago Giovanni da Verrazano and then Henry Hudson sailed their small ships into what each thought was a pretty nifty harbor. Verrazano went only as far as the Narrows, where there is now a bridge with his name, and Hudson went up the river that bears his name.

However, more time would pass before the harbor—which had a few physical problems—would become a great port. For example, the entrance from the Atlantic Ocean past Sandy Hook, a narrow spit of shifting sand, was too shallow for heavy ships. The entry from the Long Island Sound (known as the back door) into the East River was a navigator's nightmare through an estuary of conflicting currents and hidden rocks that sunk so many ships it was named Helegat by the Dutch (see chapter 5). The British preferred the name Hurlgate for the way it tossed their ships around. Tides in the East River, which is not a river at all but a tidal strait, run more swiftly than those in the Hudson. However, the currents in the Hudson flow one way in shallow depths, and another way deeper down. Needless to say, navigating the harbor safely involved lighthouses, harbor pilots, and a few people with vision and determination who made some physical alterations. But that would come later.

Early Dutch settlers erected Fort Amsterdam on a site now occupied by the old customs house at the foot of Broadway on Manhattan Island. The English didn't alter much except to rename Fort Amsterdam Fort George. In 1764, the Colony of New York built Sandy Hook Light, which at the time seemed to offer the best guide for ships entering the harbor but it was easily captured by the British. During the entire Colo-

Portrait of Colonel Jonathan Williams (1750–1815) with Castle Williams in the background, oil on canvas by Thomas Sully, 1815

nial period, despite several proposals for fortifications more formidable than the small blockhouses serving as lookout and signaling stations on either side of the Narrows, the harbor was wide open to attack.

General George Washington tried to assure the Continental Congress that he would protect New York harbor to prevent the British from sailing up the Hudson River and thus, the corridor north through Lake Champlain to Canada. If seized by the enemy this could isolate New England from the other colonies. Washington had no illusions about the difficulties he faced and worried about the number of ships that might appear and how, with no naval strength other than a few small boats with oars, he could defend a city with a very large harbor that could easily accommodate the largest fleet imaginable. Because of winds and tides, ferryboats between Manhattan and Brooklyn often had great difficulty. Even with several men pulling at the oars, crossing the mile-wide East River to Brooklyn could take more than an hour. The Hudson, or North River, as it was also called, more than two miles wide, was a still greater challenge to keep closed to the enemy.

Washington's worst nightmare occurred in early summer 1776, when the British armada sailed into New York harbor followed by more ships in the sea beyond the Narrows. It took all day for them to come up the harbor under full canvas, colors flying, guns saluting, and sailors and soldiers on the ships and on shore cheering riotously.

In his book *1776,* David McCullough gives a vivid description of the continuous oncoming British invasion. "In addition, another 3,000 British troops and more than 8,000 Hessians had arrived after an arduous three months at sea. Nothing like it had ever been seen in New York. Housetops were covered with 'gazers' and all wharves that offered a view, were jammed with people. The total British armada now at anchor in a long, thick-cluster off Staten Island numbered nearly 400 ships large and small, 73 warships, including eight ships mounting 50 guns or more. As British officers happily reminded one another, it was the largest fleet ever seen in American waters. In fact, it was the largest expeditionary force of the 18th century, the largest most powerful force ever sent forth from Britain or any nation." Such a display of sail power would not occur in New York harbor even when more than 200 years later, the first OpSail parade of tall ships from around the world entered the harbor.

The British attacked across the Narrows, landing troops on what is today South Brooklyn, Sunset Park, Bay Ridge, and Fort Hamilton, and defeated the Americans in the Battle of Long Island (also known as the Battle of Brooklyn). Washington didn't have a chance, so he very carefully withdrew across the East River in total darkness and in silence to join the rest of his army in Manhattan and then regroup in New Jersey.

AN ENGINEER IN TRAINING IN FRANCE

Meanwhile, the man who would become known as the father of the United States Army Corps of Engineers was working in France with his granduncle Benjamin Franklin. Jonathan Williams, then twenty-six, was born in Boston, the son of Jonathan Williams, patriot and merchant, and Grace Harris Williams, daughter of Franklin's sister, Anne. He was educated in Boston schools and Harvard University and in 1770 at age twenty, went to London to complete his education under his uncle's tutelage and study at Napoleon's alma mater, the French naval academy, *École Militaire*, established in 1750.

Williams had a privileged position as his uncle Franklin was widely admired in France. His image appeared on medallions and snuff boxes and his unpowdered hair and plain Quaker clothes were chattered about as what would today be considered "reverse chic."

Once war began Williams was commissioned as commercial agent at Nantes on the Loire River, then the largest port in western France, the largest slave trading port in Europe, and the European headquarters for managing the War of Independence. Williams's task was to carry out the orders of the Continental Congress to help supervise the shipment of supplies and arms to America. The commissioners in Nantes were, in effect, the secret committee set up under the leadership of and financed by Robert Morris, with the task of buying arms, supplies, and ships to aid in the Revolution. These commissioners formed an uneasy alliance and generated enough intrigue to make a James Bond movie seem like a Disney cartoon. Edward Bancroft, an American physician, who, by the way, used invisible ink, was a spy for Franklin and the committee, and later became a double agent spying for Britain as well.

Williams apparently got caught up (unwittingly) in a controversy between two of the commissioners and resigned his position as agent, but remained in Europe engaged in various business ventures and duties along with Franklin's only grandson, William Temple Franklin, until they all returned home in 1785.

During his time in France, Williams also kept the founding fathers apprised of activities in Europe, and whenever possible, sent General Washington a gift, such as a case of Margaux wine and a very handsome pair of French epaulets, which were considered treasures.

All was not work, however, and in September 1779, Williams married Marianne Alexander, daughter of William Alexander of Edinburgh, a longtime friend of Benjamin Franklin. Originally from Scotland and London, Alexander, a banker, had since moved to Germain-en-Laye, a suburb of Paris, with his family that included five daughters. Jonathan and Marianne were married at the Dutch ambassador's home in Nantes in the presence of Uncle Benjamin. In letters to Jonathan's father, Franklin described Marianne as "a very amiable young lady, who will I am persuaded make him a good wife and a pleasing companion as her conversation is very sensible and engaging." (Williams had had an earlier relationship that produced a son Josiah, but little more is known about it.)

SETTLING IN PHILADELPHIA

After the war Jonathan and Marianne settled in Philadelphia, then the nation's largest city. They would have three children, Alexander, Henry, and Christine, and later buy a house from Benedict Arnold called Mount Pleasant on the Schuylkill River. Arnold lived there for only a short time before escaping to Europe to avoid prosecution for treason. Considered one of the nation's architectural gems, the house was built by John McPherson, a colorful Scottish sea captain and patriot, in the Georgian style with Palladian windows. It is an elaborate example of eighteenth century building and carving in America's architectural history. Williams and his family lived there for two decades and eventually his children sold it to Fairmont Park, where it became a dairy providing fresh milk and ice cream to city children. The mansion is now a historic monument restored and administered by the Philadelphia Museum of Art.

Philadelphia served as the temporary United States capital from 1790 to 1800 while the permanent home was being constructed in

Washington, DC. It was also the center of the American "Enlighten-ment," populated not only by the founding fathers, but by most of the movers and shakers of the day.

Williams worked as judge in the court of common pleas in Philadel-phia and served at different times as secretary, councilor, and vice presi-dent of the American Philosophical Society, founded by his granduncle, whose members included those enlightened thinkers. Williams, who had a bright, inquisitive mind, enjoyed the stimulating company of his peers. He was also inspired by years of working with his uncle, who loved sci-ence and had already invented the lightning rod.

Thomas Jefferson was interested in Williams's plan for using a ther-mometer in navigation as a way for ship captains to know when they were sailing into the Gulf Stream without having to rely on the stars for navigation. Williams and his uncle most likely tested the waters when on their voyages across the Atlantic Ocean. While navigators identified the Gulf Stream by use of the stars and currents, Williams figured out a way to locate it by testing the temperature of the water.

"By ascertaining the relative heat of the sea water from time to time, the passage of a ship through the gulf stream, and from deep water into soundings, may be discovered in time to avoid danger, although owing to tempestuous weather it may be impossible to heave the lead or observe the heavenly bodies."

Williams sent a copy of his "Memoir on the Use of the Thermom-eter in Navigation" to George Washington and every other founding father. It was first presented to the American Philosophical Society at its November 19, 1790, meeting and was being prepared for publication in Philadelphia in 1792. Williams later published a book on the subject, which can be found today in rare-book stores for thousands of dollars.

Aside from his interest in such things, Williams had a growing family and needed to earn a living, and publishing was not a profitable enterprise. He took on some assignments in Europe, and Marianne's letters—she always addressed him as "My dearest friend"—kept him apprised of his growing children, and their friends and neighbors the city's founding families, Wharton, Biddle, and Rush. Sometimes they exchanged letters in French. There is a large collection of correspondence rich in anecdote at the Historical Society of Philadelphia. There is also a great deal of correspondence with Marianne's Alexander relatives in Europe, whom Williams mostly likely visited while he was sometimes assigned to work there.

THE FIRST SUPERINTENDENT OF WEST POINT

In 1802 President Thomas Jefferson asked Williams to be the first inspector of fortifications and subsequently superintendent of the newly established West Point Military Academy. Secretary of War Henry Dearborn, who interviewed Williams for the new post, took less than 30 minutes to offer him the job.

Williams tried to model the academy on France's *École Militaire* and the more recently established *École Polytechnique* that provided instruction to officers and cadets in the principles and applications of mathematics and engineering. However, he got little support from Congress. When Williams requested new books on science, he was put off with the excuse that scientific thought was changing so fast that they would soon be useless. There were old and outworn buildings, quickly constructed during the war when the property served as a fort, unsuitable for classes, which sometimes had to be held in dorm rooms.

Williams hated West Point and complained mightily to Jefferson. Coming from a city with a vibrant intellectual and social life, he found West Point isolated and dull and was most likely bored to death there. He also believed the academy should have been established in Washington, DC, rather than here in the country away from the activity of a city. However, George Washington had chosen this strategic location as his headquarters as well as a fortress during the war and assigned the Polish hero Thaddeus Kosciusko to design the fortification, famous for its iron chain crossing the Hudson River to prevent British ships from going upstate, or downstate to New York City. The Continental Army had hastily built stone and gravel forts and redoubts (small enclosures outside the main fort), but once the war was over Williams (who had translated some of Kosciusko's military papers for Washington) found the buildings unsuitable, and felt there was no reason to keep a military academy on such a site.

"Experience has shown that in every point of view this place is an improper one. It wants even decent society in the hours of relaxation. It wants convenience of every kind, buildings, the vicinity to a market and the means of obtaining any comfort except the coarse supplies of a contractor and every article is brought at 20 percent higher than in New York. There is not a horizontal line of 400 yards to be found unimpeded by mountains; all practice in gunnery is therefore impossible, except point blank practice with small pieces: We are so completely out of sight of Congress that one half of that body do not know that we exist at all and the other half are ignorant of our situation."

Williams left West Point after one year because of a dispute over rank and authority, but Jefferson sent him back in 1805 as lieutentant colonel and chief of engineers. On his second appointment, Williams, a proud man, got as much curriculum established as he could, but after a few more years said to Jefferson, "I have labored eight years to produce a system of military education which I wished to disseminate among all our youth throughout the Union and have barely produced a skeleton of the plan I had in view." He then added: "I am tired my dear sir, heartily tired, and although I never wished to terminate my labors but with my life, I must in future be excused from meddling with the military academy, unless by some means or other, I can see a prospect of producing some benefit to my country, and pardon my vanity, some honor to myself."

That would come soon. (West Point would struggle for a few more years until Colonel Sylvanus Thayer, who is considered the father of the Military Academy, pulled things together into what West Point is today.)

SURVEYING NEW YORK HARBOR

Since the end of the war, America's economy grew steadily and New York harbor was usually full of merchant ships with goods for buyers in Europe. By the end of the 1700s, nearly one third of all the revenue collected by the federal government was collected in New York. Being located directly on the Atlantic Ocean gave the city an advantage over Philadelphia and Baltimore and New York was on its way to becoming the main port on the eastern seaboard. Robert Fulton made his first steamship voyage in 1807 on the Hudson and by 1838, steamships would cross the Atlantic.

However, the British left New York in 1783 without fully accepting either defeat or America's independence. After all, they had spent seven years enjoying the benefits of this natural harbor and were certainly aware of its potential for their own nation. Tense relations continued, while France kept reminding the new nation of the importance of harbor defense. People who remembered that occupation of the harbor during the war worried that New York could once again be attacked. The original small fort at the tip of Manhattan known as the Battery had since been turned into a park. While the harbor became the most important one in the United States, it remained defenseless.

Jonathan Williams had long believed that New York would again be attacked by the British, who didn't like losing this prize colony and were still being aggressive to the new nation. He had ideas on what needed to be done to prevent another attack from the harbor, and he was well known in the city. Even while stranded 60 miles upriver in the boondocks of West Point, he most likely managed an occasional steamboat trip down the Hudson. He was friendly with Mayor DeWitt Clinton, who became a member of the Military Philosophical Society branch Williams had established in New York to provide some intellectual stimulation in his life away from Philadelphia.

Defending the harbor was up to the state, and Governor Daniel Tompkins, a Staten Islander elected in 1807 and in 1810 personally, took on the task of providing defense of the harbor. President James Madison appointed Tompkins commander in chief of the third military district, which included New York. DeWitt Clinton, an arch rival of Tompkins, also appealed to New Yorkers to come to the defense of their city, emphasizing the geography that made it so likely to be attacked. Clinton, largely responsible for obtaining funding to create the Erie Canal, which soon would be under way, understood the importance once the canal connected the harbor to the Great Lakes and became the gateway to the West.

In 1807 Williams was hired by Selah Strong, then chairman of the Committee of the Corporation of New York. (Strong and his wife, Anna, were infamous members of George Washington's spy ring on Long Island during the Revolutionary War.) He was assigned to inspect the entire harbor to determine the best places to erect forts. In his sixteen-page report, Williams described the depth, coastlines, and treacherous places in the harbor. He had access to old charts the English had prepared describing the channel around Red Hook, Gwoan's (Gowanus), Yellow Hook (Bay Ridge), and Robin's Reef in the Narrows, a mile off Staten Island.

Some officials thought simply lining the shores with batteries and gun stations on all the wharves would be sufficient. In time of trouble, simply call out the militia and citizens to arm the stations. Williams wanted a "great force of batteries at the entrance of a narrow passage," which "should be applied at the moment a ship comes within cannon shot, and by a powerful, quick and intersecting fire, do her all possible injury, before she comes at right angles with the battery."

"With our wharves lined with cannon, we might save the city," Williams wrote, but this kind of defense should never be relied on, as a sure protection." He reminded them that repeating this procedure over time would be, in effect, more expensive than constructing permanent batteries.

"Those who object to permanent defense because it will require time and expense and will agree to no expense that does not imply immediate effect, may spend their lives in talking upon this subject, but they will never do anything. Engineers do not deal in magic; there must be sufficiency of time, money, with a very good stock of patience, or their works will never do any good to the public, nor credit to themselves. If this harbor and bay were in possession of any one of the belligerent powers of Europe, their engineers would pronounce it to be perfectly defensible, but they would require a good fund of the three requisites before mentioned, money, time, and patience."

Williams explained that all the gun boats and torpedoes everywhere were not nearly as effective as strong fortifications at the battery, where arms could be fired in every direction to stop any ship entering the harbor. "Every sportsman knows the difference between a bird flying towards him, and one flying across his view," said Williams, "reliance upon any one mode might be illusory, the whole combined would certainly protect the Narrows, and insure security and tranquility to this opulent city."

At the end of his report, Williams acknowledged the hard work of his assistants, Captain Wilson who navigated the boat, Thomas Brown, Mr. Clark, seaman, and Lt. George Bomford, who was one of his recently graduated engineering students at West Point, and who became his primary aide in building the forts. Born on Long Island during the Revolutionary War, Bomford was the son of a British officer in the royal artillery. He designed heavy coastal defense howitzers that combined the attributes of the gun and the mortar to produce long-range, high-powered, anti-ship weapons. The guns were eventually used in all the new nation's port defenses and Bomford would become chief of ordnance after the War of 1812.

BUILDING THE FORTS: THE WELL PROTECTED HARBOR

Williams submitted his plans, drawings, and cost estimates, to the smallest detail. He designed masonry forts on Staten Island at the Narrows in 1807, fortifications on Bedloe's Island (now Liberty Island) and various other parts of the harbor, but it was the two large circular forts built from 1807 to 1811 for which he is remembered and that are still with us today as National Historic Landmarks despite several efforts to get rid of them. These two forts were so brilliantly designed and formidable that they never actually saw any combat. They were designed to keep the enemy away, and they did.

The larger fort was on the west side of Governors Island, so named during the colonial period because it was the meeting place of the region's royal governors. (The native people called it Paggank, or "Island of Nuts"!) Later named Castle Williams, this defensive work of red sandstone with walls nine feet thick was considered a prototype for new forms of coastal fortification. Williams was inspired by and very well versed in the modern French thinking on fortifications. It is circular and could project a 320-degree arc of canon fire from bomb-proof rooms on three levels.

The Southwest Battery was built on an artificial island off the Battery, as a complement to Castle Williams. It stood in about thirty-five feet of water and was connected to the mainland by a long timber causeway with a drawbridge. It had twenty-eight guns situated on one tier. In 1817 it was renamed after DeWitt Clinton, who had been mayor of New York City from 1803 to 1815. When landfill later expanded the boundaries of the Battery, the castle ended up on mainland, where it is today.

When the War of 1812 actually began, Williams asked for but was denied command of Castle Williams because of political differences with Secretary of War William Eustis. He resigned and became a brevet brigadier general of the New York state militia. Most of the activity in New York during that war occurred upstate, around Plattsburgh and Sackets Harbor, but many historians believe that the forts constructed to protect the harbor actually did their job. The state of the art fort on Governors Island inspired countless such forts across the country. You could shoot in every direction; go face to face with ships.

By 1814 the city was defended by 900 pieces of artillery and 25,500 men. That year, when five British war ships were spotted off the coast of Sandy Hook, nobody panicked. The ships never came any closer. Perhaps the intimidating nature of the castle convinced the British to avoid New York harbor altogether in the War of 1812 and attack Washington, DC, instead. The one hundred canons went unfired except for a half day of target practice.

GOING HOME TO PHILADELPHIA

During his time working at West Point and in New York harbor, Williams was cheered by Marianne's frequent letters, many of which are addressed to him at 40 Broadway, which may have been his headquarters near the Battery while the construction was going on. Williams's correspondence, reports, and papers of this period are housed in the Indiana University library archives.

During a three-month period in the winter and spring of 1811, there were numerous letters, mostly about their children, with an underlying anxiety from Marianne about their oldest son Alexander, who following in his father's engineering footsteps, had chosen to enter West Point rather than attend Dartmouth, as his brother Henry did. Given all of her husband's complaints about West Point over the years, Marianne was understandably worried that her son was in a cold and isolated area. Did he have enough warm clothing? "I want to hear about Alexander. When do you think of going up to West Point? Fanny brought my little trunk in which Alexander's engineer's coat is and I wish I could find an opportunity of sending it to you before you go to West Point that you might take it up to him." Marianne took this letter to the post herself, in order to get it on its way. In another letter, she said their daughter Christine was sending off a packet of supplies to Alexander. Marianne asked about joining Jonathan on his next trip to visit Alexander. In May she asked if he has heard from Alex since his last visit to their son. "I hope he is not sick."

Their daughter Christine, who married Thomas Biddle, had been suffering since giving birth to her first child, Clement. "After you left us on Monday and Tuesday, Christine was very sick. We moved her into our room and made Mr. Biddle sleep upstairs that the maid and myself might be with her in the nighttime. The child has not suffered but is fretful for want of its usual nourishment and therefore required more than common attention."

The Mount Pleasant house, Marianne wrote, was "in very good order but the grounds want some attention and the asparagus beds have been wholly neglected; the peach trees too are almost all dead." She wrote about the cost to replace their own carriage horses Bob and Holly.

After a brief trip home in April 1811, Williams wrote to his wife and daughter about the pleasure of steamboat travel from Philadelphia to New York. John Fitch had developed a steamboat service from Philadelphia in 1788 going to Burlington, New Jersey, and later expanded to New York via the Delaware and Raritan rivers. "This steamboat does not make the horrible noise the others do, being smaller," Williams wrote. He found it clean and "the amenities equal to the best hotel in the city" and "perfect civility attends you from all quarters."

Finally, when the forts were finished, Williams was able to go home to his family and friends in Philadelphia society again. He took up his duties as vice president and corresponding secretary of the American Philosophical Society. Alexander graduated from West Point in 1811, assigned to the engineers. He was made first lieutenant in 1813 and commanded Fort Mifflin, on what is now known as Mud Island in the Delaware River, near Philadelphia.

In the fall of 1814, when he was sixty-five, Williams won election to Congress, but it was a shallow victory for, just two months earlier, he had lost his son Alexander, only twenty-four, at the war's bloodiest and most protracted battle at Fort Erie on the Canadian and New York border. Alexander had decided, like many young men his age that he wanted to see more active duty than he found at Fort Mifflin. He advanced to captain of artillery on March 17, 1813, and was then assigned to the campaign on the Niagara frontier. At Fort Erie he was repelling the fourth assault of the enemy in hand to hand combat. When a lighted portfire— or fuse—used to set off a cannon was directed on his company, Alexander jumped forward, cut it off with his sword and was killed by a musket ball.

With all that Williams had done to protect New York harbor from the British, he was unable to save his oldest son from that war. Williams himself died several months later before he could take his seat in Congress. The cause was gout, but it may have been a broken heart.

Marianne died a year later.

Christine had five more children, one named for her brother and another for her father.

Henry graduated Phi Beta Kappa from Dartmouth and practiced law and for a time served at the head of the Bank of Scotland. He married Julia Rush, grew quite wealthy and lived to be eighty-five.

POST SCRIPT: HONORING THE FATHER OF THE ARMY CORPS OF ENGINEERS

In the end, the father of the Army Corps of Engineers was allowed his pride, and both castles remain in New York harbor despite many attempts to demolish them.

Castle Williams was used as a prison for Confederates during the Civil War, then as a regular prison, which became overcrowded and deadly. With as many as 1,100 prisoners inside, there were outbreaks of typhoid, measles, and other infectious diseases. In 1895 it became known as Alcatraz East, with newspapers reporting on the escapes attempted by swimming a quarter of a mile across Buttermilk Channel to Brooklyn. Nobody knew quite what to do with the castle. The first time it faced demolition was at the end of the 1800s, but in 1901 Secretary of War

Elihu Root, who also worked hard to modernize the Army, made a commitment to preserve the castle and overruled Army leaders who wanted to demolish it.

The Coast Guard took it over in the 1970s for storage and as a community center for their families living on the island. It was in serious disrepair and in 1972 it again faced demolition, but was saved this time by being assigned to the national register of historic places. The Coast Guard left in 1996 and the castle became a National Historic Landmark. Part of Governors Island, including the Castle, is maintained by the National Park Service, the remaining land is operated by a nonprofit organization. Park Service rangers give guided tours of Castle Williams during the summer, when the ferry operates between the Battery and the island.

The Army gave up Castle Clinton in 1821 and two years later it became an entertainment complex known as Castle Gardens, with a beer garden, exhibition hall, theater, and opera house. It also served as an immigration center until Ellis Island was built; then it served as the New York Aquarium. In 1939, city planner Robert Moses who made a career destroying historic houses and neighborhoods to build new highways, proposed tearing down the castle to make way for a new bridge connecting the Battery with Brooklyn. This caused outrage from many quarters of the city, including from Eugene Moran (see chapter 2), then head of the Rivers and Harbors Committee of the Maritime Association of the Port of New York, who rightly claimed it would ruin the Battery and lower Manhattan. President Franklin Roosevelt personally intervened and the project was abandoned. Later the Brooklyn Battery Tunnel (now the Hugh Carey Tunnel) was constructed to provide a highway from Manhattan to Brooklyn.

After the aquarium left and moved to Coney Island, politicians again called for demolition of Castle Clinton. This time concerned citizens rallied to save it and in 1946 it received National Monument designation. Today it sits proudly in Battery Park, a solid reminder of our past and the protection it provided. It serves as the ticket booth for Statue Cruises, the company that runs tours of the Statue of Liberty and Ellis Island. There are daily tours with National Park rangers and a small one-room museum on the site. However, there is no mention anywhere of Jonathan Williams.

2

The Irish Navy, Part 1:
The Moran Family

He has a great variety of upper-class clothing, much of it quite rakish, and dresses with country-club precision even if he's only going across the harbor with a barge full of fertilizer. Stokers have been known to crawl up for a look at him, after rumors of a particularly catchy ensemble, and then, much stimulated, crawl back and stoke like crazy men.
—"THE ELEGANT TUGMAN" BY ROBERT LEWIS TAYLOR, *NEW YORKER* MAGAZINE, NOVEMBER 10, 1945

TO SAY THE IRISH HAD A LOT TO DO WITH MAKING NEW YORK A GREAT maritime port is no blarney! Not only did they do most of the towing, they did most of the digging for the Erie Canal, which made New York harbor the gateway to the West. In fact, it was because relatives here said "the Irish have most of the jobs in the ditch" that Thomas Moran, a sixty-one-year-old unemployed stone mason from Kill Lara, Westmeath County, Ireland, brought his family to America in 1850.

It was Thomas's second oldest son, blue-eyed, black-haired Michael, who had the vision and the big dreams while driving mules along the canal towpath. By the time he was twenty two he was operating his own towboat. Then, at twenty-seven, with his savings in his pocket, Michael said goodbye to his family and told his sweetheart he would be back to get her. He traveled down the Hudson on a grain barge with the dream of opening a towing brokerage office in a port teeming with shipping. For ten dollars a month, Michael rented a desk in a bar at 14 South Street and Moran Towing was born in New York harbor. Today it is the largest marine towing and transportation company on the East and Gulf coasts.

THE COMMODORE

Before Michael Moran brought order to the chaos of towing, tug pilots hung out at Fisher's Saloon on South Street waiting for private tipsters (usually Western Union agents) to bring tidings of an incoming vessel. They would race to the mouth of the harbor for an approaching ship and wage a bidding war through megaphones. Sometimes it got physical, with tug crews tossing shovels, frying pans, and anything else they could find to quiet their competitors. Michael decided tug men might do better by banding together instead of battling on alone and soon he was handling towing for nearly twenty ship captains. He worked long hours and drove a hard bargain but gained a reputation for honesty. He soon bought two secondhand tugs of his own.

After years working with mules, Michael had developed a certain style of toughness to get through men's stubborn habits. If he found his crew drunk and brawling, he would grab them and bang their heads together, while quoting scriptures and admonishing their behavior. Michael was also impatient with profanity and ordered his crews to find substitutes for strong language. Experiments with "shucks" and "drat" didn't last. While Michael would brook no nonsense, he was described as gracious and compassionate. "No effort was ever spared to help anyone who needed whatever he had," his grandson Edmond J. Moran said years later.

Business was good but Michael's life was not yet complete, so in 1862 he went upstate and married Margaret Haggerty in St. Mary's Church in Albany. He brought her back to an apartment in Red Hook, Brooklyn, near the Atlantic Docks where his tugs were kept. As his family expanded, Moran bought a house at 107 William Street (now Pioneer Street). Michael and Maggie had a daughter and five sons, each son virtually weaned in the pilot house. Eugene, born in 1872, was the third

Michael Moran, 1832 1906, founder, Moran Towing

child and would eventually run the company. His brothers were Richard, William, Joseph, and Thomas, whose son Edmond would later succeed Eugene as head of the company. Agnes married J. Frank Belford, who came to work in the company.

Michael was good to his family and a question he proudly asked of the South Street cronies he brought home for dinner was: "How do you like my crew?" The first brand new tug, the *Maggie Moran*, was named for his wife, which began a tradition of naming them first for his children, then nieces and nephews. The *Maggie*, which cost six thousand dollars, was the first to carry the now famous white block letter "M" on its smokestack. "It was a great day for father and mother, as it was for us kids, when the tug was commissioned in 1881," Eugene later wrote. "We climbed and poked over every nook of the vessel." Sadly, Maggie Moran died two years later at age forty-two of a lingering illness. Three of their sons would also precede Michael in death. Richard died of consumption at twenty-six. Thomas died at thirty-nine and William at twenty-seven.

Michael was of medium height but his large frame made him appear bigger. He wore a black coat, kept open and a heavy watch chain with a small compass bounced over his belly. "In his blue eyes a twinkle was usually lurking," recalled his son Eugene. "He laughed a good deal." His charm and savvy kept Michael on the good side of Tammany Hall at a time when New York was the largest Irish city in the world. He got the exclusive contract for moving the city's garbage out to sea. A few years later, Moran tugs would tow away the excavated rock from the city's first subway tunnels. Although a staunch Democrat, in 1896, Michael was so adamant about the danger of William Jennings Bryan's fiscal ideas, that he put posters and banners all over his tugs urging votes for the Republican William McKinley for president.

In preparation for the celebration of the opening of the Brooklyn Bridge in 1883 (see chapter 6), Michael directed the tugboat patrol to see that the docks or ships were not set ablaze by the massive fireworks display. His son Eugene remembered standing on deck with his father later to watch the "heavenly display."

At the 1883 centennial of the British evacuation of New York, Michael was designated the honorary commodore for tugs in a big marine parade. The title stuck and fellow boatmen began calling him the "Commodore of the Irish Navy."

THE DEAN OF THE HARBOR

Michael's son Eugene may have been the most colorful of the Morans. This dapper little leprechaun—the press always described what he wore—became a huge influence on the events of the harbor. In 1921 he was appointed a commissioner of the new Port Authority of New York and he played a leadership role in all the port's maritime organizations. He quickly established himself as a marine oracle and gave the impression that he owned the harbor and was only letting others use it. Nevertheless, his opinions were carefully considered because he was usually right. He encouraged development, raised a ruckus when anything threatened the harbor, like putting La Guardia airport on Governors Island, or Robert Moses idea to connect Brooklyn and lower Manhattan with a bridge rather than a tunnel. And he protected the harbor, too, understanding even then, the importance of wetlands to the health of the port.

In his youth, however, Eugene did not foresee this future. His heroes were seamen and he wanted to work on the tugs like his brothers. With little interest in school, and after much pleading, his father gave him the chance to start at the bottom with no special favors. At fourteen he went to work with Peter Cahill, his father's friend and business partner, who loved to sing "Rock of Ages" at the top of his lungs while piloting the tugs. As it happened, the day Eugene reported for work, the cook failed to show up, so he was drafted right into the galley. The only dish Eugene knew how to make was ham and eggs, which he sprinkled generously with brown sugar. This went on for three days when the captain threw in the towel. "We got to get some different grub. This crew's tough but they are looking a little peaked around the gills." Eugene then went to the store for some bacon and canned beans, but he was urged by all aboard that perhaps there was some other job better suited for him. He also worked as a deckhand, but Michael recognized that his son was too small for the muscular work and had a better aptitude for the administrative end of the business.

Eugene had endless curiosity and the energy to go with it. He learned all the different jobs in the company and knew everyone who worked there. He was no less involved in social and church activities and at twenty-five married the equally vivacious and popular Julia Claire Browne. They had two sons and four daughters.

By the beginning of the twentieth century, the Moran Company had tugs working all along the Atlantic coast. In 1905 the company was incorporated with Michael, seventy-three, as president and Eugene, now thirty-four, as vice president. Michael's son Joseph, several nephews, and a son-in-law, also worked in the company. In 1906, the year of Michael's death, the company moved from South Street to the new Whitehall building at 17 Battery Place at the tip of Manhattan with its wide-angle view of the entire harbor. The building had a narrow ledge on the twenty-fifth floor where orders could be shouted through a six-foot megaphone to the tugboats in the harbor below. Nothing thrilled Eugene more than to be up there watching Moran tugs pushing and pulling all over the harbor.

This may have inspired him to help organize a marine pageant in the harbor for Theodore Roosevelt's return in 1910 from his world tour. Many said it was the best show ever seen in the harbor, which the former President must have deemed "bully."

At the end of World War II, when the *Queen Mary*, carrying troops back from Europe, was spotted approaching the harbor, Eugene grabbed a pair of binoculars, according to the *New Yorker*, "and with his white hair flying, ran like a deer up six flights of stairs to the roof."

In 1917, Franklin Roosevelt, then secretary of the Navy, commissioned Eugene a lieutenant in the Naval reserve because he knew more about New York harbor than the Navy did. He was part of a three-man committee to quickly assemble a fleet of small craft for the British, who badly needed patrol vessels. Eugene also chaired the Joint Committee on Port Protection, which kept a sharp eye out for sabotage. He even helped capture a German spy living at Sandy Hook, New Jersey, by watching a suspected house. When he saw a plume of sparks shooting up from the chimney, he notified the officials, who found a hidden telegraph. Eugene was promoted to lieutenant commander.

The media loved Eugene Moran, not because of his maritime expertise or vocal opinions. They loved his style. Here's what Robert Lewis Taylor wrote for a 1945 two-part profile in the *New Yorker*, "The Elegant Tugman":

"The president, who is five feet five inches tall, has white hair parted on one side, and a permanent look of impish gaiety. As a result of riding tugs in all kinds of weather, and of using a sun lamp, his face and hands are fashionably tan. He has a great variety of upper-class clothing, much of it quite rakish, and dresses with country-club precision even if he's only going across the harbor with a bargeful of fertilizer." The writer continued, "Stokers have been known to crawl up for a look at him, after rumors of a particularly catchy ensemble, and then, much stimulated, crawl back and stoke like crazy men."

On his eightieth birthday, the *New York Times* ran the headline: "Moran 'Too Busy' to Mark Birthday. Now 80, Tug Chairman and Dean of Harbor Still Has Many Irons in the Fire." Even in his retirement, Eugene went to Port Authority meetings twice a week. Occasionally he would host officials from other countries who wanted a harbor tour on a tug.

In 1945 Eugene was happy to give Walt Disney a tug tour while Disney was researching his animated movie, *Little Toot*, based on the classic children's book about a baby tug who doesn't want to work in the family business. Eugene also wrote a book with Lewis Reid: *Tugboat: The Moran Story*, published by Charles Scribner's in 1956.

After his wife died, Eugene bought a house in Bay Shore on Long Island, where his family had summered for years. He liked to fish from his thirty-six-foot cruiser, *Off Shore*, on Great South Bay. For relaxation he read history, biography, and mysteries, stimulation for an inquiring mind that didn't call it quits until the age of eighty-nine.

The Admiral

Company leadership passed to Eugene's nephew and Michael's grandson, Edmond J. Moran, described as mild-mannered with a ready smile. Like his uncle, he was short and somewhat barrel-chested. Edmond had been working since his school vacation days on the tugs. He never wanted to do anything else and worked his way up the company from office boy to president. He was proud of his pilot's license and often took the wheel when aboard one of his tugs. "We in the tug business think of our tugs as the propelling power behind the complex machine that is New York," he said in a 1965 address to the Newcomen Society. Edmond lived to be ninety-six and worked in the company for sixty-nine years.

As a World War I Navy reservist, Edmond returned to action when World War II began. Admiral Harold Stark, commander of the US Navy in Europe, met with Moran about how to land one thousand tons of supplies directly on the beaches. Edmond knew what they needed and where to find it, leading them to harbor railroad car floats and shallow draft gasoline barges. These craft had not usually ventured out of New York harbor, but they were successfully sent in convoy with some small tugs across the Atlantic, escorted by military ships.

Considered one of the greatest experts in tugboat operations in the world, Edmond was selected by the American and British navies to plan how and when to deliver two artificial harbors, known as mulberries, to Normandy to support the D-Day invasion troops. This idea was scoffed at until Edmond said it could be done and proceeded to do it. He assembled and coordinated a fleet of more than two hundred tugs from American, British, French, and Dutch fleets. He circulated among tug crews on the British coast, refining plans, moving equipment, keeping morale high. He organized the largest fleet of tugs ever assembled and ninety massive concrete structures, described as the eighth wonder of the world, were towed across the English Channel.

For this heroic deed, newly named Rear Admiral Moran received (among others) the US Legion of Merit, the French Croix de Guerre, and the Order of the British Empire. Perhaps the most rewarding honor came in 1944 when an American Liberty ship was named for Michael Moran. The whole family went to the Maine shipyard for the launch followed by a lobster picnic. The ship was christened by Nancy, one of six children of Edmond and his wife, Alice Laux, who were married for sixty-three years.

After the war Moran Towing had its greatest development as Edmond guided the expansion from Maine to Texas and inland on the

Great Lakes and the Mississippi and Ohio Rivers. In 1947 they made history with the longest single tow of 12,996 miles from Tampa to the East Indies with two huge mining dredges.

Continuing the family tradition of service to the industry and the community, Edmond served three terms as president of the Maritime Association of the Port of New York and New Jersey and was on the board of managers of the American Bureau of Shipping. He served as a trustee of the Museum of the City of New York, vice chairman and board member of Fordham University, and a director of the South Street Seaport Museum. Edmond also served as a director of Mystic Seaport Museum, and a chairman of India House, the famed maritime dining club in lower Manhattan. In addition, he served as police commissioner of Darien, Connecticut, where he lived.

In 1964, the Admiral's eldest son, Thomas, took over the presidency for the next thirty years, but the company was losing its family domination. Eugene's two sons had retired, and his grandson, Eugene III, left in 1980.

In 1973, the company moved from Battery Place into the fiftieth floor of the yet to be completed World Trade Center. Then, in the early 1980s, they moved to Greenwich, Connecticut. With operations all over the country, there was no longer a need to be headquartered in New York. The passion of the early Morans was ebbing, and to expand, the company began to look outside the family. In 1994, shortly before Thomas died, he sold the company to the Barker and Tregurtha families and his youngest brother, Edmond Jr.

THE LAST MORAN

Edmond "Ned" Moran Jr. is the youngest son of the Admiral, twenty years younger than his brother Thomas. After graduating from Georgetown University and serving in the navy, Ned began working in Moran sales in 1971. He moved to finance and accounting, then managed company operations in Jacksonville, Houston, and Baltimore, before coming back to headquarters. As senior vice president he is in charge of all harbor operations out of New York, as well as corporate sales and marketing and new business development.

Ned is proudest of the Moran contributions to the government during times of crisis. During the Spanish-American War, the first American vessel in Havana harbor was the *M. Moran*, a tug chartered by James Gordon Bennett for his *New York Herald* reporters. In addition to the service of both world wars, Moran also towed cargo to Da Nang for the navy during the Vietnam War.

Like his ancestors, Ned Moran has carried on their history of service. He is past chairman of the Board of Directors of the American Waterway Operators, a trade association representing the nation's tugboat and barge owners. In 2004 he received the US Coast Guard's Distinguished Public Service Award, their highest honor given to civilians, recognizing his efforts in improving towing vessel safety in the United States. In 2015 he was appointed to the Marine Board, a branch of the Transportation Research Board of the National Academy of Science. He was also a pilot commissioner for the State of Florida, helping to regulate and license harbor pilots. Ned was a member of the Board of Trustees of Bryn Mawr School, as well as the Board of Visitors of the Georgetown University School of Business.

While Ned may be the last Moran in the namesake company, he has not lost his interest in the family lore. As a boy he sailed on his father's sloop *Kill Lara*, a name taken from the town where the Morans came from. But when Ned visited Westmeath years later, he could find no such town as Kill Lara, and no record that stonemasons had ever worked in Westmeath.

Whether or not that mystery is ever solved, there are now six generations of Morans—hundreds of them around the world—from the family of Michael Moran. They are teachers, bond traders, journalists, photographers, and real estate lawyers. In Ned's own family, his daughter Amy is a clinical social worker at Johns Hopkins Medical Center. His son Ned (Edmond J. III) is a software engineer in Washington, and daughter Meg is an art consultant in Washington, DC. Ned's wife, Judy, who was his college sweetheart at Georgetown and has worked as a nurse and psychologist, is a family law professor at the University of Baltimore.

Not a tugboater in sight. Nevertheless, tugs with the big white M are still pushing and pulling in New York and a dozen other harbors.

Moran Clan Reunites for a Day in Brooklyn

On a fine autumn day in September of 2010, seventeen Moran descendants and their spouses from as far as Luxembourg and as near as a few blocks gathered for a reunion and bus tour of the Brooklyn neighborhoods where their ancestors had lived. They began with 107 Pioneer Street (now Warren Street) in Red Hook, where Michael Moran lived when he founded Moran Towing more than 150 years before. Everyone received a lapel sticker with the family crest: three golden stars under the name Moran. A color printout of more than a dozen homes of Morans past was provided by Diana Moran Charbier, daughter of Joseph Henry Moran. Her husband Wilfred served as tour guide.

Eugene Dwyer from Virginia handed out a printed Moran genealogy, while his brother Tom from Connecticut offered a map of south Brooklyn, with Moran homes noted. For thirty-eight years, their sister Doris, the eldest granddaughter of Eugene, has lived in Texas, where she serves as a nun with the Daughters of Charity. When the Dwyers' father, Thomas, married Eugenia Moran in 1930, it connected two Irish families that had been in the maritime trade since the days of the Erie Canal.

Mike Bellford is a grandson of Michael Moran's only daughter, Agnes. Some cousins have kept in touch over the years, but a few met for the first time on the bus. Ned Moran had never before met his Luxembourg cousin, W. Dirk Warren, a grandson of Eugene. Passing the entrance to 47 Plaza Street near Prospect Park, Dirk recalled his boyhood visits with his grandfather. As sponsor of the day's event, Dirk was nattily dressed in a gray suit with a blue and pink brocade vest and striped tie, perhaps a sartorial inheritance from his grandfather. Dirk served with the US Army in Europe during World War II and fell in love with Elz, which is why he lived in Luxembourg. He served as Luxembourg's consul to the principality of Lichtenstein. Elz and their daughter Beryl joined him for the reunion.

Peter Moran, another grandson of Eugene, moved to Maine after a career in finance and service on the board of Moran Towing before it was sold. His siblings, Mike and Marie, were also on hand with their spouses, identified on labels as MBMs (Morans by Marriage).

The lone tug man, Captain John Cray, sporting a handlebar mustache, flew down from Portland, Maine, for the day. Cray's grandmother was Eugene's sister Agnes Moran. Cray began working for Moran's East Coast operations and later left to become a pilot on his own and a consultant on tug or piloting operations. Ned told the others how Cray helped settle the tug strikes of the 1980s. "If he had not done that, the company would have been very different in the last thirty years."

There was much reminiscing on the bus. Tom pointed out the house on Third Street where he was born, while his brother Eugene got up to photograph each house. Passing Methodist Hospital, Nick Moran, a great-grandson of Eugene's brother Thomas, said his son, now eight, and a sixth-generation Moran, was born there. Ned, of the fourth generation, said he was born there, too, but many years earlier.

Most of the Morans had left Brooklyn behind by 1945, but composer and guitarist Nick Moran moved into the Prospect Park area by chance. He did not realize until Diana contacted him about the reunion how many of his ancestors had lived in the neighborhood. At the end of the tour, the bus dropped off the Morans at the 1888 landmark Montauk Club in Park Slope, where all posed for a group photograph before sitting down to lunch. Peering down at them from the wall was a large 1939 framed photo of the duck pins bowling club reunion with Eugene and his brothers front and center.

"Seventy years ago," someone pointed out, "earlier Morans were upstairs having Bloody Marys."

Author's Note: Since the reunion, Captain John Cray and W. Dirk Warren have passed away. This chapter is an updated and expanded version of articles originally published in *Irish America* magazine.

3

The Irish Navy, Part 2:
The McAllister Family

My father said in 1974, you'll never make it. You have no reserves to fall back on.

— CAPTAIN BRIAN MCALLISTER

WHEN BRIAN MCALLISTER WAS GROWING UP IN BROOKLYN IN THE 1950s, he was more interested in playing basketball than in higher education or pursuing the family business. "Learning was not on my agenda," he quipped. However, over the years, he became the heart and soul of the business his Irish ancestors built and he fought hard to keep it from sinking out of the hands of future generations. Today McAllister Towing is one of the nation's largest towing companies, with operations in ports all over the East Coast and Puerto Rico. Captain Brian McAllister, now in his eighties, still occupies his office at the tip of Manhattan overlooking the harbor where so much of his family's history happened, but he has passed the management on to his two sons and two nephews, now steering future generations along in the family trade.

THE FATHER OF THE LIGHTERAGE BUSINESS
The story began in 1864 when James McAllister, 22, left Cushendall, County Antrim, in Northern Ireland to seek his fortune in New York, then the largest Irish city in the world. Working his way across the Atlan-

tic as a mate on a ship that ultimately wrecked off the coast of Labrador, James continued his journey until he eventually arrived in a thriving port that handled more goods and passengers than any other in the world. Many Irish immigrants worked as longshoremen, loading and unloading ships, and lighterage work, a backbreaking occupation, was also widely available. Lighters, similar to large barges, then operated by sail, ferrying cargo and people between moored ships and docks, piers, and railheads. James found such work on Newtown Creek, which separates Brooklyn and Queens and empties into the East River. According to legend, this business so inspired him that he took a higher paying job as a mate with the Ward Line on a merchant ship headed for Cuba so that he could earn enough money to start his own lighterage business.

Meanwhile, Catherine Reid came over from Ireland in 1867 to marry James, and the couple raised four sons and six daughters in their brownstone home at 161 India Street in Greenpoint. James, who became known as "Whiskers" for his long beard, began with a single-sail lighter, which he refitted from a sloop, and established Greenpoint Lighterage Company. He built the business by transporting and distributing barrels of kerosene and oil between the eighteen refineries that lined the shores of Newtown Creek and ships around the harbor. John D. Rockefeller, already known for his ruthless tactics against competitors, owned one of those refineries—the first one built in New York—and reportedly offered McAllister a substantial piece of the company if he would put his fleet of lighters at his service in exchange for stock in the new Standard Oil Company. James said no.

Once established, James summoned his brothers Daniel and William along with two brothers-in-law from Ireland to join him as partners. In 1876 they bought a shipyard on Newtown Creek, and the company's first propeller driven tugboat, the *R. W. Burke*, began operating. They also maintained an office across the East River at South Street, where most harbor business was handled.

After eighteen years of marriage, Catherine died of tuberculosis, in 1885. Her funeral was held at St. Anthony's Roman Catholic Church on Metropolitan Avenue. More than 150 carriages of mourners lined the streets to pay their respects to the now well-known McAllisters. Four

Captain Brian McAllister, chairman, McAllister Towing
COURTESY MCALLISTER TOWING

years later James married twenty-six-year-old Catherine McDonnell, a cousin of his first wife. They lived at 1294 President Street in Brooklyn and had three children.

As the busiest port in the world, New York was the scene of international action including shipping arms to support the Cuban struggle for independence from Spain. James had strong sympathy for the Cubans and according to an 1896 story in the *New York Times* a McAllister lighter had been found alongside the steamship *Bermuda,* operated by the notorious harbor pilot and gunrunner Dynamite Johnny O'Brien (see chapter 4). When federal agents came to the McAllister home, James denied he was hiding guns and refused to let them in without a search warrant. However, his eight-year-old daughter Florence, known as Flossie, peered out from behind her father's legs and said, "Oh poppa, they are upstairs in the bathtub."

James's sons from his first marriage grew up working in the business, along with an assortment of cousins and other relatives. James Patrick, the eldest son, who would become known as Captain Jim, joined the firm when he was sixteen. A few years later he eloped with Isabel Stulz, who would be known as Belma to her grandchildren. In time they moved to 1510 Albermarle Road, Prospect Park South, a neighborhood that would be home to the McAllisters for much of the 1900s.

One day near the end of the century, Captain Jim stormed out of the South Street office to go into business for himself around the corner from his father and uncles, but the family soon reunited to form McAllister Brothers in 1897. In 1900, they moved into new offices at Broad Street in lower Manhattan. (They stayed in this general area until moving in 1955 to their present location at 17 Battery Place.) However, they had neglected to sign papers and formally divide up the shares. Captain Jim and his uncles clashed frequently about this over the next four years, and one day decided to meet on board one of the tugs and not return to shore until the issue was settled. A.J. (Brian's father), then six years old, recalled going with his dad to a pier where he was told to wait until his father returned. It was getting dark, and A.J. was greatly relieved when he finally saw the tug return. Captain Jim, his face covered in blood, jumped off, grabbed his son's hand and said, "It's settled."

The shares were redistributed making Captain Jim the leader of the second generation.

Captain Jim was always finding ways to promote the company and in July 1914 offered use of the tug *JP McAllister* to Harry Houdini, the famous escape artist who had himself handcuffed and sealed into a packing case, and tossed into the harbor near the Battery. Miraculously, a few minutes later, he surfaced, free of the packing crate and his handcuffs. The story made all the newspapers.

The McAllisters did a great deal of business with John H. Starin, an innovator in marine transportation as well as a two-term US Congressman. Starin had developed the car float, a barge with tracks for carrying railway freight cars across the harbor and McAllister tugs transported these car floats for years. When Starin died in 1909, the McAllisters bought his fleet of excursion steamboats that ran to Coney Island, the Statue of Liberty, and Bear Mountain despite objections from Captain Jim, who felt the passenger business was too risky. In case of an accident you could always replace lost cargo, but passengers were another matter. He may have been thinking of the 1904 *General Slocum* steamboat disaster in the East River, when the boat caught fire and more than a thousand people burned to death or drowned. Nevertheless, the excursion business flourished for the McAllisters until the automobile became the preferred mode of recreational travel.

After a series of strokes and four years of declining health, James McAllister died in November 1916, at the age of seventy-three, at his President Street home. He was buried in Calvary Cemetery on a knoll overlooking Newtown Creek, where his first wife was buried. A line of horse carriages stretched from St. Anthony's Church three blocks along the streets. Family members as well as Greenpoint neighbors and the maritime community, joined the funeral cortege across the Manhattan Avenue Bridge over Newtown Creek. The *Brooklyn Daily Eagle* called James McAllister the "father of the lighterage business in the port of New York." James left the towing and lighter business to his sons from his first marriage and the steamboat business to his two brothers. His second wife, "Black Kate," and their children were not part of the business but received James's extensive real estate holdings and cash.

CAPTAIN JIM, THE INNOVATOR

Driven and intense, Captain Jim was the opposite of his father in temperament. While James McAllister was "the reserved Irish gent who measured his words," his son was described as "a man of brain and brawn, with a keen intellect and a strong set of arms and two big fists." Fiercely competitive, Captain Jim swore he knew the New York waterfront better than anyone, which was probably true because he was the only civilian asked to sit on the Board of Embarkation for the government and served as acting director for the army's floating equipment during World War I. Allies needed the US to supply food, goods, and ammunition, and McAllister Brothers was filling the need.

Always an innovator, Captain Jim continued to grow the company in new directions his father and uncles could not have imagined. For example, anticipating the need for lighters to carry oil in bulk rather than in barrels, he had earlier convinced his father to convert a number of his sail-lighters into bulk-oil carriers by creating built-in tanks. He led McAllister to diversify into deep-sea salvage, towage, tanker operation and even hunting for sunken treasure. He was described by one family member as the sparkplug who kept the company expanding into new ventures.

By 1918 the company moved into the ocean towing business, operating one of the first deep-sea tug barge combinations running molasses between New Orleans and Cuba. Profiting from industry high periods, McAllister tripled the size of its fleet with tugs and barges. Always active in maritime affairs, Captain Jim served in 1922–23 on the board of directors for the Maritime Association of the Port of New York and New Jersey.

In 1922, New York's Mayor Jimmy Walker called Captain Jim to see if he could pick up Eamon De Valera, who had arrived by steamer in Hoboken to do some fund-raising in Manhattan for the Irish nationalist cause. A.J., then just out of his teens, was sent along to escort De Valera. More than thirty years later when A.J. and his wife Marjorie passed by Parliament House on a visit to Dublin, he asked the guard to extend his compliments to the then Prime Minister. To A.J.'s astonishment, De Valera remembered him and asked the couple to come around later for a visit. "If I heard this story once, I heard it twenty times," Brian said. "This was the highlight of his life, I think."

As an adult, A.J. along with his brother J.P. (James Patrick II) worked full time at McAllister Brothers. A.J. was a mechanical engineer by training, with a degree from Stevens Institute of Technology in Hoboken. Like his dad, he was inspired by innovation. Diesel engines were the new big thing and he wanted to surprise his dad by installing a four hundred horsepower diesel engine in the *Daniel McAllister,* making it the first diesel-powered tug in New York harbor. Surprises did not sit well with Captain Jim who would have preferred to be consulted on such a serious matter, so he fired his son. However, A.J. took his mother's advice and went to work the next day as though nothing had happened and all was fine. Everyone knew they needed to convert to diesel, but it would take some time.

Captain Jim lived to see the business triple in size and then get hit so hard by the Great Depression that their credit was exhausted and they had to sell off their fleet until they were down to one remaining functioning tug. Harbor commerce and traffic came to a standstill, docks deteriorated, and by 1932 world trade eroded to half its previous volume. Captain Jim advised his sons to look for work somewhere else. He was only sixty-six when he died in 1935 from a coronary occlusion. When Brian asked what caused his grandfather to die so young, his father told him he died of a broken heart.

The Third Generation: Pulling Themselves Up from the Great Depression

Three sons of Captain Jim, J.P., A.J., and Gerard, along with a few cousins, kept the business afloat by reorganizing and some taking outside jobs. (Although some daughters did work in the company offices from time to time, true to the era, they were not given any management responsibilities.) Once again, however, the brothers and their cousins had to find ways to settle their differences about ownership, but the sons of Captain Jim managed to keep control.

It would take the next world war to turn things around. Once again, New York harbor was handling more ships than any other port and the majority of merchant shipping. The harbor was also the principal embarkation point for millions of troops. Because of their track record with the military in World War I, McAllister got a contract for moving munitions and explosives—as much as thirty thousand tons of ammunition arrived every day by rail—through the harbor, dangerous work given the threat of explosion and the presence of German U-boats outside the port. Lighterage crews transferred the cargo to barges; then their tugs towed it to Gravesend Bay in Brooklyn where it was loaded onto military ships. By the end of World War II, Brian's dad and his two uncles had thirty-five tugs running, even though they were mostly secondhand older wooden-hulled steamboats needing repair. They leased additional boats as needed.

"After World War II, Moran had sealed up 70 percent of the ship business in the harbor. That was enormous," Brian said. "McAllister, with thirty-five tugs on hand, had maybe 15 percent." He said they were all highly competitive and engaged in price wars. Rather than building new boats, the McAllisters preferred to buy up other tug companies, not only for a flotilla of quality tugs but also acquiring some of the best crews and docking pilots in the harbor. (Docking pilots, highly trained and licensed, take the reins from the ship's captain while it is docking. Harbor pilots, on the other hand, guide the ship as it enters or leaves the harbor. Both pilots operate at the discretion of the ship captains.) McAllister purchased Russell Brothers towing company and its subsidiaries and then Dalzell Towing Company and began operations in other regions. Building the company back up in the 1950s and 1960s, they were operating sixty tugs in ten ports.

Shipping and transportation went through great changes in the postwar years as the as newly constructed interstate highway system meant trucks were replacing lighters. Piers and other structures around harbor were in decline as New York's master planner, Robert Moses, began through his various state and city positions to surround the waterfront with highways, bridges, and tunnels. While the tugs carted some of the materials needed to build these structures, they looked for new ways to survive as much cargo was now trucked under and over the harbor.

The suburban sprawl that developed with the new highways, however, offered other opportunities. The McAllisters got back into the business of transporting people, this time across Long Island Sound. It acquired the New London Freight Lines, a passenger car ferry between New London, Connecticut, and Orient Point on Long Island. They followed this with the Bridgeport and Port Jefferson line, to help the company's long-term survival. There was also a family connection to the area. In 1921 Captain Jim bought a home in Belle Terre overlooking Port Jefferson harbor, a place still in the family, and where reunions are sometimes held.

THE FOURTH GENERATION ON THE BRINK

Brian was born on Christmas Day in 1932, one of eight children and grew up in his grandfather's house on Albemarle Road, near Prospect Park in Brooklyn. His father, A.J., would take all the boys to the shipyard. "I was scared to death on the boats," Brian said. When he was twelve or thirteen and working as a summer deckhand on a tug, he recalls his fright at watching the very tricky task of maneuvering one ship from a line of three and then moving another ship into the same slot. He told the pilot he was scared. "I gotta get out of here," he said and was sent to the engine room. "I was happier down there," he said because he didn't have to watch what was going on. Despite Brian's alleged lack of interest in learning, he attended State University of New York (SUNY) Maritime College at Fort Schuyler. When he was about to be drafted, his father insisted he get serious about completing his bachelor's degree in maritime engineering, which he did in 1956. Then he served until 1958 as an executive officer on an LST 880, a naval tank-landing ship, with the rank of Lieutenant JG.

Next he piloted for the American Export Isbrandtsen Line, making a lot of money. "I loved it," he said, but also realized he was spending too much time away and asked his father for a job on the tugs.

By the 1970s Brian said his dad was not in good health and only three of Captain Jim's eight children were in the business. "My uncles didn't have all their kids in the business," he added. (There are now close to one thousand descendants from the original James McAllister, but most of them drifted away from the family business into other areas. Those in the business today are descended from Captain Jim and his sons.)

Brian's father and uncles, the third generation, wanted to sell the company so that they could retire and take their equity with them. The fourth generation had no choice but to buy their parents out or watch the company be sold to strangers. Brian knew that emotionally they never wanted to sell out, but they had practically no money other than the value of the company itself. When Brian realized they were close to selling the business for $20 million, part of which was stock in a Canadian company, he told his father he wanted to find a way to keep the business in the family. "My father said in 1974, you'll never make it. You have no reserves to fall back on." He told Brian they couldn't buy a company with 100 percent debt and no working capital.

"I was a fairly aggressive guy, although I didn't know much about finance," Brian admitted. He knew in his heart that their careers and lives would be fundamentally diminished and the legacy of McAllister Brothers lost if the company were sold to an outside interest. He persuaded his brothers and cousins to put up $3,000 each and form a corporation, McAllister Towing and Transportation, in order to buy the old company.

Brian invited a Harvard MBA to help with the financial arrangements and come aboard as a partner. He felt his financial expertise was crucial to closing the deal and the fourth generation bought the company from the third generation for $20 million in 1974. The third generation didn't think the fourth generation could make a go of it, but Brian, then forty-three, was determined. For four years they struggled with overwhelming debt and teetered at least once on the brink of bankruptcy in the 1980s. Brian wanted to hold onto his and the company's heritage. This resulted in a lawsuit for control and in 1998 the company was divided, with the Harvard MBA partner taking the oil business they had acquired and Brian keeping the towing and ferry business. The settlement was made one day before the company was to be auctioned off. By now Brian's sons, Brian "Buckley" and Eric, were providing their combined expertise in law and finance. By 1990 the company was functioning quite well. McAllister Towing and Transportation has been called the "Rocky" of the tugboat business. And Brian McAllister is a true hero.

THE FIFTH GENERATION: KEEPING IT IN THE FAMILY

After surviving a 2005 heart attack, Brian decided it was time for the fifth generation to take over. Buckley McAllister took over as president of the company, a position Brian had held since 1984. Eric is vice president and chief financial officer. Captain A.J. McAllister III, Brian's nephew, is senior vice president of sales, while another nephew, Andrew McAllister, is vice president of IT. Like Brian, A.J. graduated from SUNY Maritime College at Fort Schuyler and is a licensed docking pilot and master of ocean towing.

Buckley's early experience on tugs, like his father's, was less than comfortable, when he worked during high school and college vacations. One year, he experienced a storm off the Florida Keys and he decided that perhaps staying in school was not a bad idea. He graduated from Hamilton College cum laude in 1989 and University of California, Hastings College of Law in 1993. He went on to practice law for four years in California and got married there. He and his wife, Beth, and son Rowan temporarily moved back into his old room at home to help his family hang onto the company. Eric graduated from New York University with a degree in economics, had worked in the Commercial Equipment Finance Division of GE Capital, and was assistant treasurer of Carolina Barnes Capital, Inc.

Brian, a vigorous man, is chairman of the company, and while he no longer plays basketball, he enjoys golf and tennis whenever he can. He also likes to walk to work from the Manhattan apartment he shares with his wife of nearly fifty years, the former Rosemary Owens, who taught math at the United Nations International School in New York when they met at a birthday party given for Brian's father. Rosemary was his younger brother's date!

Brian still comes to work and the delight he takes in his family and the family business is infectious. The McAllister corporate office on the twelfth floor of the historic landmark Whitehall Building, 17 Battery Place at the tip of Manhattan, affords a stunning vista of the upper bay. The Statue of Liberty seems close enough to touch, and the iconic orange Staten Island Ferry passes regularly as do the small commuter ferries and the McAllister tugs with their distinctive red stacks with two white stripes. History is proudly on display throughout the offices in paintings, photos, and models of tugboats.

Today, more than 150 years after James arrived from Cushendall, McAllister is still not as big as Moran, but unlike Moran, the company is still in the family. Will the sixth generation carry on the family trade? It's too soon to tell, but if it's any incentive, they all have had tugboats named for them. Buckley's teenage son Rowan works as a deckhand during school recesses, while his younger sister Janet worked a summer job in the office as Brian's assistant.

With more than eight hundred employees and eighty-five vessels operating out of seventeen locations, the $170 million annual business today is 73 percent ship assist, 20 percent ferry, with the remainder split between ocean towing and miscellaneous projects, such as marina and terminal operations, oil barge movements, leasing, emergency response, and towing construction materials.

The port itself has changed drastically during that time, as passenger ships gave way to airline travel, and container ships replaced break bulk freighters, but the port is also more environmentally healthy and so are the tugs, which have evolved from coal-driven to diesel to Z-drive tractor tugs.

On September 19, 2014, McAllister celebrated their 150th anniversary at a gala event at Chelsea Piers (once used by ocean liners) complete with a tugboat birthday cake. And in 2015 they published a 250-page book written by Stephenie Hollyman, filled with stories and photos of their history, *150 Years of Family Business: McAllister Towing*.

4

Dynamite Johnny O'Brien:
A Captain Unafraid

He was tricky, like fog. You knew he was there, but you couldn't locate him. He tantalized and mystified the Coast Guard. He would use the most obvious maneuver, sailing in the open water—it was part of his outguessing technique.

—EUGENE MORAN, 1956

JOHNNY O'BRIEN WAS ALREADY FAMOUS AMONG SAILORS FOR HIS extraordinary skill as a harbor pilot guiding ships through the treacherous waters of Hell Gate in New York harbor. But when he outmaneuvered Spanish gunboats and United States Revenue cutters to keep the Cuban rebels supplied with weapons and supplies in the 1890s, he became a legend. His waterfront cronies often accused him of not only starting the Spanish-American War, but of keeping it going. The Cubans believed Johnny O'Brien was responsible for freeing them from four centuries of Spanish oppression and they gave him a lavish birthday banquet every year for the rest of his life.

O'Brien was a short man with a thick gray handlebar mustache and the proud stance of a buccaneer. But there was no bravado about him, a *New York Tribune* reporter wrote. "He is one of the most daring and clear-headed that ever lived, a man with a hair-trigger intelligence that enabled him to act as swiftly as he could think."

GROWING UP IN THE SHIPYARDS

Johnny O'Brien was born on April 20, 1837, near the East River. He often said it was in the shipyards of the Lower East Side, where he learned to spin oakum and wedge treenails into boats. From the 1820s to 1900, the city's dry dock area, from Grand Street north to East 12th Street was lined with ships under construction. The area, near the shore, Avenues B, C, D, later known as Alphabet City, was home to dockworkers, mechanics, and shipbuilders, many of them Irish immigrants. Johnny's father worked as a machinist, reportedly at Brown's Shipyard at the foot of 12th Street, where George Steers designed the famous yacht *America*, which would launch the America's Cup.

Johnny's parents, Peter O'Brien and Bridget Sheridan, were farmers from County Longford, Ireland. Johnny claimed the Civil War general Phil Sheridan was his cousin, his mother being the sister of the general's father. Both families came from the same part of Ireland and allegedly

Hand-drawn image by John O'Leary
TROUBLE OR FORTUNE FILMS, COPYRIGHT 2016

arrived on the same boat. It was said Sheridan was born at sea, but his birth has always remained a mystery partly because he and his mother insisted he was born in Albany, New York, where the family stopped on their way to Ohio.

Young Johnny learned to sail and navigate on his older brother Peter's ferry—a large rowboat with a sail—crossing the East River to Greenpoint in Brooklyn. Johnny was so intoxicated with the sea that his parents finally let him leave home at thirteen to sign on as a cook on a fishing sloop. He eventually piloted fishing and sailing yachts, served as apprentice on the pilot boat *Jane*, and spent time on a Union ship during the Civil War.

A DAREDEVIL AND A FAMILY MAN

At thirty-one, Johnny married Josephine Nodine of Brooklyn, a good-natured woman ten years younger than her husband. They made their home in Arlington (now Kearney), New Jersey. It was a chaotic and happy household with eight children—five sons and three daughters— born between 1870 and 1890. Despite his clandestine activities and long absences, O'Brien described Josephine as "the best wife in the world," who supported his activities. With a growing family, O'Brien wanted to stay close to home for a while (although that did not mean settling down, he insisted). Being, as he admitted, "constitutionally disposed to giving orders rather than obeying them," he took the required training in navigation at the Thom School on Cherry Street for a command rank as a pilot in the Hell Gate Pilots Association.

In his pilot "uniform," dark suit, vest, white shirt, bow tie, and black hat, O'Brien would take over for the ship's captain before they entered Hell Gate and shout orders to the crew as he guided big windjammers past barely visible rocks and swirling eddies while the clearly tense captains stood by. "See if you can get a dollar bill there between the beam and the rock," O'Brien liked to tease. Once the windjammer was out into Long Island Sound, a pilot boat came alongside to take O'Brien back through Hell Gate and the East River to South Street to await his next assignment. Eventually he became known as "Daredevil Johnny" because while he appeared to be taking chances, he always got through without a scratch to the ships. He knew when he could pass safely within a foot of the shore. He knew where the wrecks were, as well as every sign of tidal change in that treacherous estuary. (See chapter 5.)

The Name Dynamite Sticks

O'Brien's colleagues began calling him Dynamite Johnny rather than Daredevil Johnny in 1888 when, at the age of fifty-one, he was hired to carry sixty tons of dynamite to Panama in a seagoing yacht. *Rambler,* the largest schooner in the New York Yacht Club, was purchased by a Cuban businessman who allegedly had some interests in coal mining in Panama. Finding a crew willing to sail with sixty tons of dynamite was not easy and it troubled O'Brien to be less than truthful about the cargo. The Cuban reminded him that he had the same problem finding a licensed ship's master. O'Brien quipped: "Well, being Irish, I have a natural affinity for dynamite."

Anchored off Liberty Island in the middle of a summer night, the gaslight glow from the new statue's torch was the only illumination on the water. Three smaller boats tied up alongside and several men in dark clothing unloaded hundreds of fifty-pound boxes of dynamite onto the schooner. In the hold of the yacht, O'Brien pried open some of the boxes to be sure the dynamite sticks were properly packed in sawdust.

All went well until they encountered a powerful electrical storm in the Gulf of Mexico. Quickly they reefed in sail against the wind as rain fell in solid sheets. The crew was awestruck at the spectacular streaks of fire in the sky, but O'Brien was terrified. If lightning struck the tops of the masts it would go straight down into the hold and start a fire. He kept discreetly quiet about the cargo, as a mysterious current ran through the vessel. His hair crackled like a hickory fire when he ran his hand through it. Whenever a man handled a piece of metal, he got a shock. O'Brien noticed a man trying to light his pipe during a temporary lull. He rushed over and tossed the man's matches overboard and walked away without a word. As dawn came up, the storm subsided, and they were again sailing in a beautiful trade wind. That was the first and last time he ever lied to his crew.

Admiration for José Martí and Cuba Libre

The Cuban struggle for liberty attracted O'Brien, who had known and admired José Martí, the rebel leader and poet who operated from a New York waterfront office during the 1880s and '90s and "who could tell a story as good as any Irishman." When Martí was killed in 1895, on an arms expedition off Florida, he was replaced by Tomás Estrada Palma, sixty-one, a thoughtful and polished man who ran a school for boys in Central Valley, New York. Now an American citizen, Palma had sworn never to return to Cuba. After much resistance, he agreed to take over Martí's job as head of the junta. Horatio Rubens, twenty-seven, a brilliant Jewish-Cuban American attorney and trusted friend of Martí, provided legal counsel to the revolutionaries. In other words, he helped them avoid prosecution by American and Spanish authorities, and kept them out of jail. The junta formed a new "Department of Expeditions" and asked O'Brien to become the official navigator. They would pay him $300 for each trip, the equivalent of about $8,500 in twenty-first-century dollars. However, O'Brien insisted that in addition, they send his wife $100 a month.

O'Brien was already a known associate of the Cubans and had made several successful filibusters (gunrunning) for them. The Cuban liberation movement was popular in New York, where many Cubans worked in cigar factories as well as other jobs. The leaders of the junta found a base of support and sympathy and raised considerable sums of money to buy arms and other supplies to take to the Cuban rebels. O'Brien knew everyone in New York harbor and found many sympathizers in the maritime community. The Spanish government knew of this clandestine activity and paid Pinkerton detectives to spy on the junta, and particularly O'Brien. At the same time, the US government had to keep tabs on him, so the navy as well as "revenuers" (US Treasury Department agents) were always looking into his activities. The city's newspapers helped the cause as well by fanning the flames about the atrocities being done to the Cuban people. William Randolph Hearst's *New York Journal* and Joseph Pulitzer's *New York World* were particularly avid in sensationalizing the cause in what became known as "yellow journalism." The public devoured newspaper stories of these daring "filibusters" by reporters like Richard

Harding Davis and Stephen Crane. So reporters as well as spies and government agents kept tabs on Johnny O'Brien's activities.

HIDING IN PLAIN SIGHT

Early in his filibustering career he outran the Coast Guard in his home port. "I used my outguessing technique," O'Brien liked to say. One night in an early gunrunning expedition, "we slid from our pier on South Street on the East River without lights, started down the river and crossed to the Brooklyn side. It was black out, and I could hardly see," but as O'Brien often said, "I know the harbor as intimately as my wife's face." If an alert lookout for the Coast Guard spotted someone moving, he would report, "I'll bet it's Dynamite Johnny on the run," so a cutter was sent out to check both shores.

"I saw the cutter steaming up the river, its lights twinkling in the murk. They knew we was [*sic*] there, but they couldn't find us," O'Brien said. "They knew they should stop me, but I think they were half-hearted about it. I was breakin' the law, but all the people felt the Cubans should be helped." It was obvious to O'Brien that the safest place to hide would be the Navy Yard itself—in among other ships in various stages of construction or refitting, including the beautiful USS *Maine,* newly built there. "The Coast Guard would never think of looking for me in this cove in the Brooklyn shore. Sure enough, as the Coast Guard cutter raced up the river to nab us, I made my way out of our shelter and went in the opposite direction. Moving rapidly downstream, through Buttermilk Channel and hugging the shore off Bay Ridge, we was [*sic*] soon through the Narrows, heading south."

In another expedition in spring of 1896, the steamship SS *Bermuda* was tied up at an East River pier all day as lighters brought cargo marked as codfish and medicines to be loaded as tugs with reporters and spies hovered nearby. There was much coming and going of past and present crew, meant to confuse the spies and reporters, but no one was told when the ship would sail. O'Brien came aboard at night to check the new boilers and perform engine repairs with trusted crew members. After questioning the remaining crew, he paid off those he did not trust. Then he left and spent the night at a rooming house near the Battery.

Meanwhile, on the United Press tugboat docked within sight of the *Bermuda,* reporters compared notes. One claimed that O'Brien took out clearance papers for Veracruz with a load of codfish, but another said that if O'Brien was involved, they would be going to Cuba. Reporters who had gone to the O'Brien home to find out where Dynamite Johnny might be were told by his son Jack that they never knew exactly where their father was but he always turned up if they'd care to wait. The tugs with reporters and US marshals waited around until the *Bermuda* cast off. However, when the ship left the pier, it dropped anchor in the harbor near the Statue of Liberty.

The house in Arlington was also watched constantly by detectives hired by the Spanish government. One night, O'Brien's wife Josephine, threw a pot of boiling water over one of the snoops who ventured onto the porch to eavesdrop under the window. His son Fisher suggested a way to beat the detectives at their own game. When O'Brien was followed from the house, Fisher would follow the detectives and once in Manhattan, find a way to let his father know where they were lurking. If O'Brien had no crucial meeting with the Cubans, he might confront the Pinkertons and buy them a drink.

During the night a tug brought O'Brien and a fireman aboard the Bermuda and as they steamed out of the Narrows, two press tugs came tearing after them, reporters firing questions through megaphones. A third tug, hidden until now and hired by Pinkertons, joined the chase but as a blizzard blew up outside Sandy Hook, the tugs gave up and went home.

The Spanish government, in an attempt to stop O'Brien's activities, sent a representative to the O'Brien home in January 1897 with a letter offering O'Brien $24,000 to reveal the location of the next expedition. (This hefty sum, the equivalent of more than $600,000 today, indicates the desperation of the Spanish.) After asking a few questions, O'Brien folded the letter and simply stared at the man, who went away thinking he had a deal. The next day at the junta office, the Cubans locked the document O'Brien brought them in the safe and, at the right time, would leak it to the press.

DAUNTLESS, COMMODORE, AND *THREE FRIENDS*

Martí's successors raised money to buy arms and also charter three powerful seagoing American tugs designed especially to transport supplies
and ammunition to the Cuban rebels with O'Brien in charge. The new
tugs' owners were paid $10,000 per trip, whether or not it was successful.
The *Dauntless* and the *Three Friends* were most often piloted by O'Brien.
The third tug, the *Commodore,* would later be immortalized in Stephen
Crane's short story "The Open Boat."

Rubens went to the Brunswick Navigation Company near Savannah
with 30,000 one-dollar bills to procure the *Dauntless,* 100 feet long with
525-horsepower engines and painted black as the Cubans ordered. It was
love at first sight for O'Brien and the *Dauntless.* The hold could carry
the 1,300 rifles, 100 revolvers, 1,000 cavalry machetes, 800 pounds of
dynamite, several hundred saddles, half a ton of medical stores, 460,000
rounds of small arms ammunition, and a breach-loading Hotchkiss
12-pounder. This, when assembled, resembled a small cannon, or a large
rifle on wheels.

Over the next year, there were countless expeditions carrying arms,
food, and supplies to the Cuban rebels, with much cat and mouse intrigue
between New York and Cuba in East Coast ports like Charleston, Savannah, Jacksonville, and Key West. Cargo would be switched from one tug
to another. The tugs would change directions, and set up false trails to
lead the US Navy as well as Spanish vessels off their trail. The authorities
would chase the tug they believed was loaded and on the way to Cuba,
only to discover that it was occupied in legitimate tug work. When the
navy cruiser *Vesuvius* arrived in Jacksonville harbor to keep an eye on
Dauntless and *Three Friends,* O'Brien paid a courtesy call on the captain
and afterward, took the navy officers for a ride on *Dauntless.*

O'Brien could navigate in pitch darkness to slip past blockades and
warships. He would run directly at a Spanish gunboat to force it to chase
him out into open sea and away from where he had just unloaded men and
arms. He taught the crew how to stoke the coal so only a thin, pale stream
of steam would escape the stack and avoid notice. He had tarps thrown
over the hatch covers and the binnacle light and, not least, ordered the
chain-smoking Cubans to put out all cigarettes under penalty of death.

Horatio Rubens spent a good deal of time traveling up and down the East Coast to bail out O'Brien and the other crew members of the tugs. For example, when *Dauntless* was seized by federal customs agents as soon as she arrived in Jacksonville harbor on the grounds that she had gone to a foreign port—meaning Navassa Island, an uninhabited piece of land near Haiti, for they could not prove she had gone to Cuba—on a coastwise license to transfer cargo to another boat, Rubens, much to the surprise of the government's lawyers, proved that the United States had jurisdiction over Navassa Island so *Dauntless* had not gone to a foreign port. In another case, Rubens's questioning of eyewitnesses so confused them that they were unsure of what they actually saw, agreeing that most tugs look alike.

ENRAGING THE SPANISH GOVERNMENT

O'Brien's ability to land a cargo of arms within a mile or two of a Spanish garrison in Banes Bay, near Guantanamo, enraged Spain's governor of Cuba, General Valeriano Weyler, known as the "Butcher" for his cruelty in forcing Cubans into concentration camps. Sitting at his favorite table at Café Jerezano with an aide, Weyler was asked by an American reporter about the Banes Bay incident. The incensed Weyler said, "When I capture Johnny O'Brien, I will hang him from the flagpole at the Cabanas [a fort on the eastern side of the harbor] in full view of Havana."

The reporter couldn't wait to let Johnny know about this, and Weyler got a colorful reply. "To show my contempt for you and all who take orders from you," O'Brien replied by mail, "I will make a landing within plain sight of Havana on my next trip to Cuba. If we should capture you, which is much more likely than you will ever capture me, I shall have you chopped up into small pieces and fed to the fires of my ship." A few days later O'Brien landed *Dauntless* with a cargo of explosives less than three miles from the palace of the captain-general.

The story eventually made its way to the docks and bars and homes of seamen and even into their log books. It also made the agenda at the White House. At President William McKinley's cabinet meeting of October 22, 1897, the *Dauntless* came under heated discussion because Spain's ambassador to the United States was demanding that something be done to stop the filibusters. Despite sympathy for the Cuban cause, the United States government frowned on illegal gunrunning and chased after O'Brien, who remained undaunted about breaking the law. "We were rebels once ourselves," he said.

When the USS *Maine* steamed into Havana harbor in January 1898, Captain Charles Sigsbee went ashore to pay a courtesy visit to the Spanish governor of Cuba and assure him the arrival was not an act of war. They were there to offer protection and assurance to American citizens in Cuba. Sigsbee also had orders to keep an eye out for *Dauntless*. Three weeks later, on February 15, the USS *Maine* blew up, killing 267 Americans on board. Headlines across America accused the Spanish government of terrorism.

O'Brien and his crew on *Dauntless* didn't hear about the *Maine* until they returned to Jacksonville harbor days later, but he doubted the Spanish would be dumb enough to blow up the *Maine*. A commission was set up at Havana to investigate, but Hearst's reporters had leased a Moran tug and were the first to arrive in Havana to report on what they blatantly called an act of terrorism without waiting for the investigation, and war began. In New York, paperboys shouted the headline "US Declares War on Spain." American flags flew from all the buildings. Banners with "Remember the *Maine*" were prominent in store windows all over New York and this soon became a catchphrase. And the rest, as they say, is history, as Theodore Roosevelt and his Rough Riders suited up for battle in April 1898.

US policy was to strengthen the rebels until a real Cuban army could get organized. "It may not be as much fun now that it's legal," O'Brien quipped to a news reporter after he was ordered to take charge of the *Alfredo*, the first warship of the new Cuban Navy, a sloop with a gas engine, then under construction in a Bronx shipyard. When O'Brien arrived in Key West harbor on the *Alfredo*, he got a big reception and took pride in hoisting the Cuban flag in an American city. Reporters made fun of the small size of the Cuban Navy, but O'Brien said he drew the plans himself, because he wanted a boat that matched his size. He continued to aid the Cuban cause until the war ended five months later in August.

With "filibusterin' in the dumps," O'Brien held a variety of piloting jobs and one of these took him back to Havana in May 1902. He paid a visit to his old friend Tomás Estrada Palma, now president of Cuba, who wanted O'Brien to head the Cuban Navy. However, O'Brien told them that at sixty-three he was getting to be an old man and his rheumatism was bothering him. Then they offered him a job as chief pilot of Havana harbor, but he would have to become a Cuban citizen. O'Brien refused to give up his American citizenship, so they waived the rule. O'Brien's wife and youngest children, probably daughter Helen, twelve, son Peter, fourteen, and possibly another daughter Josephine, twenty, joined him and made their home in Havana. "Piloting in Havana is as simple as transporting in New York harbor at slack water," O'Brien said, "but I like the Cuban climate."

The United States had declared war on O'Brien's birthday, which may have been one reason the Cuban government gave him a lavish birthday banquet each year. The first cake was adorned with fake sticks of dynamite instead of candles.

THE LAST SKIPPER OF THE *MAINE*

Fourteen years after it sank, the *Maine* was raised from the bottom of Havana harbor to be towed out to sea. The United States Navy apparently harbored no hard feelings about Dynamite Johnny's past illegal activities and asked him to guide the *Maine* on her last voyage. O'Brien wasn't sure he deserved such an honor, but his ego was swelled by the recent weeks of interviews with reporter Horace Smith, who was writing about his adventures for the *New York Tribune*, later to be published as a book entitled *A Captain Unafraid*. In fact, he had recently donned this same suit and white tie to have his portrait taken for Smith.

So on the eve of St. Patrick's Day 1912, Dynamite Johnny O'Brien, now seventy-five, put on his best morning suit, a starched white shirt, and a bow tie, and climbed onto the rusted and patched deck of the battleship. He put his pilot's cap over his iron-gray hair and stood beside the flag with his feet spread, the natural stance of someone who had walked on ships all of his life. Bright blue eyes kept watch from a face weathered from endless days under the Caribbean sun and its reflected glare from the sea. He had carefully trimmed his thick walrus mustache for the occasion and looked less like the soldier of fortune he had been called in the years before the war. This was a proud moment for him, as it was for the USS *Maine* and for the United States.

A dozen other men that he had hand-picked—some Cuban, some American—followed him, each one carrying bundles with hundreds of pink, red, or yellow roses. They set about rigging up a temporary mast on which to hang the American flag. Then, they made a last-minute inspection of the ship's seaworthiness, checked the integrity of the towline, and laid the roses on the deck in front of the flag. All but one left the ship.

All of Havana had turned out for the day's ceremonies and thousands crowded around the edge of the harbor. Some had climbed atop the Morro Castle walls at the head of the harbor and were waving flags and flowers. The harbor itself was filled up with American and Cuban military ships, yachts, and small fishing boats.

O'Brien raised his arm and signaled that he was ready for the navy tug *Osceola* to pull him free of the cofferdam that had been built a year ago to raise the mud-encrusted hulk from the bottom of Havana harbor. At that time, the remains of sixty-six more American sailors were found and identified, by corroded trinkets and personal effects like a bugle or a gold watch. The sixty-six caskets were draped in both American and Cuban flags and carried away to the SS *North Carolina* while guns sounded a salute. The sailors would be buried at Arlington National Cemetery where President William Howard Taft delivered a eulogy. Smaller tugs were tied to each side of the ship. Standing on the deck of the *Osceola* were the US minister to Cuba, several American generals, and plenty of navy brass.

Guns of the three forts around the harbor sounded a farewell, and the ships formed a cortege out of the harbor. Outside the harbor they encountered heavy seas and O'Brien signaled to the *Osceola* to slow speed to ease the rolling. The broken ship had been patched together with iron and concrete in order to make this journey. It was being towed stern first to keep it stable long enough to reach the open sea three miles out and laid to rest once and for all. The navy had wanted to use dynamite to re-sink the old hulk and O'Brien shuddered at the thought. It would be too terrible, a reminder of how it had been sunk in the first place. He convinced them to do it without noise or violence.

Despite a new government investigation done while raising the ship from the bottom of Havana harbor, most people still believed the sinking of the *Maine* had been an act of terrorism by the Spanish government. A few thought the Cuban rebels did it in order to force America into the war. But O'Brien knew a thing or two about dynamite and how easily it could spontaneously combust given the right conditions. The *Maine* had carried old brown powder that could disintegrate and ignite if not stored properly. Coal dust could also ignite, and O'Brien believed Charles Sigsbee, the commander of the *Maine*, had not run a tight ship.

Now he breathed the sharp salt air and felt the heavy rhythm of sea beneath him like a heartbeat. In the tow boat ahead, a motion picture camera had been set up on a tripod to record the event. They had reached the three-mile limit later than planned because of the heavy seas. It was nearly five o'clock instead of the scheduled three o'clock when around the world, others had been scheduled to join in the final ceremony for the *Maine*. In New York the thirty thousand people marching in the St. Patrick's Day Parade paused for five minutes at 3 p.m. Churches of all denominations tolled their bells for five minutes in a tribute to the dead heroes who went down with the *Maine*. All the ships at sea, tugs and ferries in harbors, too, sounded their whistles and flew their flags at half-mast. O'Brien didn't know it then, but his name would appear on page one of the *New York Times* and other newspapers. His most important piloting job did not go unnoticed.

The escort vessels formed a circle around the *Maine* and O'Brien's work party came aboard again. As sailors blew the mournful taps into the air, O'Brien and his crew opened the valves and sluice ways in the bulkheads of the hulk to let the water rush in. Captain Dynamite Johnny O'Brien removed his hat and as his hair fluttered up from his scalp, took the edge of the American flag in his hand and kissed it. He replaced his cap and climbed down the ship's ladder to a waiting launch that brought him to the Osceola. A band on the *North Carolina* played "The Star-Spangled Banner."

As the air pressure exploded between the decks of the *Maine*, a few plumes of water shot to the surface. It took thirty minutes for the ship to slip beneath the surface. The flag remained fluttering and flapping, as if to put off the inevitable, for nearly twenty minutes before sinking out of sight in the Florida straits.

"Old Glory vanished under the foam with a flash of red, white, and blue as vivid as a flame," O'Brien told a reporter. The canopy of roses drifted into an ever-widening circle. The American cruisers and Cuban gunboats sounded the final salute and filed back to Havana at a swifter pace. Another twenty-one-gun salute sounded from Morro Castle when they returned to the harbor.

The emotion of the day had pulled hard at Dynamite Johnny, too. "Someday not too far from now somebody would open my buzz cocks and let me drift into the deep," he told a reporter. O'Brien had spent his life on the water, but now the briny, brackish scent of the East River, of New York harbor, was calling him home. He would like to sit in the Moran Company's office on South Street with the tugmen again and tell them some stories. He recalled the old potbellied stove and the smell of fuel oil and grease and coffee and fish from Fulton Market. And his family had done well. He always had luck, he used to say, and he had luck with his family, most of all.

THE FINAL JOURNEY

Five years after he piloted the *Maine* to her final burial, Dynamite Johnny O'Brien complained of not feeling well, and called for his old friend, Victor Hugo Barranco, the New York special agent of the Cuban government. He said faintly, "I feel, Vic, I won't sail this ship much longer. Where's the nearest dock?" O'Brien had spent the last five years of his life in his home port, but during that time he had several strokes, was partially paralyzed, and was confined to a wheelchair. He lived in a room in the Hotel America, most likely paid for by the Cuban government. Whether his wife lived there with him is unknown, but somebody would have had to help him navigate daily life from his wheelchair. It is more likely that Josephine lived with one of their now-grown children and came to the hotel to visit and care for her husband.

O'Brien died on June 22, 1917, a few months after his eightieth birthday and the Cuban government ordered a solid bronze casket and a huge floral wreath. The funeral, led by O'Brien's fellow Masons, was held at Campbell's Funeral Home on Broadway on June 25. Josephine and their eight children were there, as well as their grandchildren, and scores of relatives and friends. Also attending were the Sandy Hook harbor pilots, and Spanish-American War veterans, some from as far as Savannah, Georgia.

Augustine Barranco, son of Victor Hugo Barranco, gave the eulogy on behalf of President Mario García Menocal of Cuba, about the man who had done so much toward freeing the island from the rule of Spain.

Dynamite Johnny was buried in Sailors Cemetery on City Island near the shore and facing the harbor he so loved. And while no bells tolled throughout the city, and Dynamite Johnny was no longer front-page news, he nevertheless was given quite a send-off. Respectful obituaries appeared in all the newspapers.

POSTSCRIPT

Dauntless served as a dispatch boat for the Associated Press during the Spanish-American War and then went into regular towing service in the southeast. Her name was changed a few times and she finally was dismasted in 1946 after fifty years of service.

Three Friends was kept by her owner, Napoleon Bonaparte Broward, who became governor of Florida in 1905. The boat was sold after his death and used to tow World War II liberty ships during a ceremony in Jacksonville. After years of neglect it sank in Jacksonville harbor.

The *Commodore* was immortalized by Stephen Crane's short story "The Open Boat." Crane, then a reporter for the *New York Journal,* was aboard the boat when it sank and was later rescued with three others after spending days at sea in a small boat.

General Tomás Estrada Palma became the president of Cuba in 1902 after the United States occupation ended, although the election itself was questionable. He was deliriously happy, O'Brien recalled, but when the government got bogged down in corruption and scandals, Palma resigned and asked the United States to intervene. He died in 1908, at the age of seventy-three, four years before the *Maine* was raised.

Horatio Rubens was made an honorary citizen of Cuba and visited the country often. He continued his law practice in New York and headed the Mantanzas railroad company in Cuba. He amassed an extensive art collection that now graces several museums in New York City. He died in 1941.

General Valeriano Weyler was recalled from Cuba in 1897, before the Spanish-American War started, because of all the complaints about his cruelty to people. He loved animals, however, and spent his remaining years in Spain among his horses. He outlived all the other players (except Rubens) and died in 1930 at the age of ninety-two.

The Republic of Cuba never forgot Johnny O'Brien and there are at least two monuments in Havana honoring him. The memorial plaque to "El Capitain Dinamita 1837–1917" is in old Havana, near Plaza de las Armas and the "los Practicios del Puerto," or the Havana Pilots Association. Although it hasn't been corroborated, there was allegedly a bronze statue of O'Brien in the harbor that was taken down by accident during the Cuban Revolution because it was thought to be a depiction of a "Yankee imperialist."

In 2014 Irish musician and filmmaker Charles Gavan O'Brien (no relation to Johnny) decided to make a film about Dynamite Johnny, called *A Captain Unafraid,* after the book title. "I first heard about Dynamite Johnny O'Brien," he said, "when I read an article by Cuban historian José Antonio Quintana called 'John Dynamite, Marine Mambi,' which means maritime rebel." Filming was begun in August 2014 in New York and later in Cuba, with the cooperation of the Union of Artists and Writers of Cuba. In the course of making the film, O'Brien and his crew interviewed twenty-five people, including this writer, who are in the film. They interviewed four sea captains, many historians, authors and maritime experts, a round-the-world solo sailor, and a gunrunning Irish priest, who for the last fifty years has lived near Johnny's childhood home, and two of Johnny's great-granddaughters who live in Little Rock, Arkansas, a great-grandson Tim Clayton in Atlanta, Georgia, as well as Stephen Barranco, a nephew of Victor Barranco, Harrisonburg, Virginia. Another descendant lives in Cuba, and is a great-great-grandson of O'Brien, most likely descended from one of Johnny's daughters who lived in Cuba with him and married there.

In April 2016 the film was released and entered into several film festivals, including the Havana International Film Festival. The filmmakers expected the film would also play at the Lower East Side Film Festival in New York as well as in Arkansas, Atlanta, Dingle, Cork, and Galway.

5

John Newton:
The Man Who Opened Hell Gate

The ship seemed as conscious of her danger as any on her decks. The bows whirled away from the foaming reef. The ship had so happily escaped the dangers of the first reef, a turbulent and roaring cauldron in the water . . . an element called "the Pot" lay directly before her. Ludlow looked around him for a single moment in indecision. The waters were whirling and roaring on every side, and the sails began to lose their power as the ship drew near the bluff which forms the second angle in this critical pass. He saw by objects on the land that he still approached the shore, and he had recourse to the seaman's last expedient. "Let go both anchors!" was the final order.
—FROM *WATER WITCH* BY JAMES FENIMORE COOPER, 1830

JAMES FENIMORE COOPER, WHO HAD EXPERIENCE ON SAILING SHIPS, got it right in this description of Hell Gate, the narrow S-shaped passage of erratic currents, a turnstile for ships traveling between the East River and Long Island Sound, which the Dutch called Helegat. The British called it Hurlgate for the way it tossed the ships around. Others called it Hell's Gate as it was indeed the gate to hell for mariners and caused so many shipwrecks that most sailors would not venture through the passage without a good supply of whisky to fortify their nerves.

General John Newton
LIBRARY OF CONGRESS

William Kornblum in his book *At Sea in the City: New York from the Water's Edge*, writes, "Early explorers like Adriaen Block clawed their way through the boiling tide rips and rockbound rapids of the Hell Gate under the power of sail and fear. They kept ship's lifeboats, anchors, and grappling hooks always at the ready." Sea captain logs as far back as the early 1700s talk about a giant whirlpool punctuated with rocks, reefs, and islands.

In 1780, while their navy still controlled the harbor, a British captain for some reason decided to take the *Hussar* through Hurlgate. The ship struck Pot Rock near the dangerous reef along the Astoria shore and after several hours of swinging around in the tides, it sank. Legend has it the *Hussar* was carrying $1.8 million in gold and seventy American prisoners. To this day, treasure hunters try to find the gold to no avail, although a still-live cannon from the *Hussar* was allegedly found in the 1980s.

Hell Gate was indeed a scary place until a brilliant engineer, Civil War veteran Lt. Colonel John Newton of the Army Corps of Engineers took on the task that it was finally cleared and made safe. And it took him nearly twenty years. Flood Rock, the largest and final obstacle was removed in 1885 with six times the greatest explosive charge ever fired in the world until the atomic bomb. Newton was so careful and so confident that he allowed his adored twelve-year-old daughter to pull the switch that detonated the explosion.

FIGHTING FOR THE UNION

John Newton was a Virginian who fought for the Union during the Civil War. He was born August 24, 1822, in Norfolk, the son of Congressman Thomas Newton, who served for thirty-two years from 1801 to 1833, and his second wife, Margaret Jordan Pool Newton. John's oldest brother, Washington Irving Newton, was a career cavalry officer in the Union Army who had studied cavalry tactics in France. A second brother, Cincinnatus, stood as an elector for Jefferson Davis, and a third brother, Thomas, is said to have traveled to California in 1848 and was never heard from again. Newton also had a half-sister, Caroline, by his father's first marriage.

John Newton was privately tutored in mathematics and engineering, in which he excelled early on. He entered West Point at sixteen and graduated in 1842, second in a class of fifty-six that included future generals James Longstreet (54th), Abner Doubleday (25th) and John Pope (17th). Newton stayed on at the Academy for three years as an engineering instructor before joining in the Army Corps of Engineers. His specialty was military architecture and for the next six years he helped build or improve forts along the Atlantic Coast and Great Lakes.

In 1846 Newton was assigned to New London, Connecticut, as assistant engineer to George Washington Cullum for the restoration and redesign of Fort Trumbull, which today is a state park. It is here that Newton became acquainted with Anna Morgan Starr, whom he married in 1848, when he was twenty-six and she was seventeen. Anna, a direct descendant of John and Priscilla Alden, was the daughter of Jonathan Starr and his second wife, Catherine Lumiere Synthoff Starr. The Starrs were prominent bankers in New London and some of their homes there are now historic landmarks. Starr Street is named for them.

In early years of their marriage, John and Anna moved around to various posts to which Newton was assigned, and when the Civil War began he was the army's chief engineer for Pennsylvania. Newton commanded a division at Antietam and then Fredericksburg. That battle led by General Ambrose Burnside was such a disaster that a handful of Union officers including Newton, tried to have the general removed from command. They blamed him for a futile frontal attack that resulted in hundreds of Union soldiers being killed, twice the number lost by the Confederates. Newton and the other officers met with President Lincoln at the White House; while it would be a breach of protocol to tell the president they wanted Burnside fired, instead, as Newton later told Congress, he emphasized "that the troops of my division and of the whole army had become entirely dispirited," and that they had no confidence in Burnside's ability to run things.

Meanwhile, at President Lincoln's urging, Burnside resigned, to be replaced by General Joseph Hooker. There were political consequences to the complaining officers, however. Some of them were forced out of the army and while Newton remained, his career suffered. He had been up for a commission to major general, which did not come through. Nevertheless, Newton fought in the Atlanta campaign with General Sherman, who thought highly of him. At the Battle of Peachtree Creek, a dangerous Confederate movement against Sherman was prevented by Newton's quickly constructed defensive works, forcing the rebels to retreat. This victory helped restore Newton's army career. He spent the last months of the war in Key West and the Dry Tortugas. (He would later be promoted to brigadier general and become the army's chief of engineers.)

TAKING CHARGE OF NEW YORK HARBOR DEFENSES
After the war Newton returned to the Army Corps of Engineers and was put in charge of New York harbor defenses and spent the rest of his life here. Initially he worked on new batteries at Fort Hamilton, Sandy Hook, and the dredging at Kill Van Kull and the Hudson River. In his long career he would advise on many important civil engineering works, including the Brooklyn Bridge, which had just gotten under way in 1869. He was one of three engineers selected by John Roebling and the trustees of the bridge to visit Roebling's other works, and also to offer their opinions on how the height of the bridge might interfere with commerce (see

chapter 6). Newton was a member of the Brooklyn Harbor Line Commission; revising external lines of piers and bulkheads on the Brooklyn side of the East River.

Throughout his time in New York, Newton gave lectures, at places such as Cooper Institute (now Cooper Union) for the benefit of the New York Dispensary, an infirmary that provided health care to the poor.

In 1866, the Army Corps of Engineers asked Newton to examine Hell Gate and prepare a plan for clearing away the obstructions. In January 1867 he began the first step, a plan for removal of Hallet's Point reef from the waters off Astoria and the subsequent removal of Pot Rock, Frying Pan, and all the other rocks and reefs and ultimately, the largest obstacle, the nine-acre boulder known as Flood Rock. To accomplish this successfully, Newton needed to solve difficult engineering problems never before attempted, and invent new apparatus, notably a steam drilling machine, which has since been in general use. At the age of forty-four, Newton began a project of unprecedented size, complexity and importance. He was flying blind almost the entire time, inventing, improvising, and ultimately succeeding. Over the nearly twenty years of work, there were eighty to as many as three hundred workers involved.

The East River is a tidal strait, a narrow saltwater passage from the upper bay that separates Manhattan and the Bronx from Brooklyn and Queens. As it reaches what is now Wards Island and Brother Island, with upper Manhattan on the west and Astoria on the east, it makes a right turn into Long Island Sound. The Harlem River flows down from the north and joins the East River at this confluence of boulders, rocks, varying depths of water, and the narrow S-curved Hell Gate passage near the shore of Astoria. As someone once said, the water surrounding the island of Manhattan moves quickly in all directions, much like its citizens on land. If you drive over Hell Gate today on the Robert F. Kennedy Triborough Bridge from Astoria Park to Ward's Island, it looks quite calm and peaceful.

Before it was cleared, all these varying depths and bays along the shores as well as the small islands and rocks in its midst created a nautical obstacle course of conflicting currents and depths. Over the years sailors gave names to all the obstacles: Pot Rock, Greater and Little Mill Rocks,

Hen and Chickens, Frying Pan, Bald Headed Billy, Brea and Cheese, the Hog's Back, Flood Rock Island, and others less suitable to print. The late Claude Rust, a writer who specialized in articles about the area, described the waters "like wild beasts, circle their confines, impatient for the chance to escape."

In early days of tugboating it was standard practice for a pilot and his crew to take on a personal cargo of rum before tackling Hell Gate with a big schooner. Wild currents and sharp bends compelled the use of eight or nine tugs on a job that in ordinary waters would require only one.

Once steamboats came into use, it was thought they would have a better time of it because they were not dependent on wind and sail. Alas, they were not safe either. Historians of the period reported that about one in fifty ships trying to run the gauntlet of Hell Gate was either damaged or sunk in the 1850s. In an average year, a thousand ships ran aground.

If Hell Gate could be made relatively safe for navigation, several ocean miles could be saved in reaching the Atlantic. Known as the back door to the port, Hell Gate was a necessary passage to reach the many ports of Westchester, Long Island, and Connecticut, and it saved hours on the trip to Boston through the calmer waters of Long Island Sound. City officials pleaded with Congress for funds to remove the obstacles from Hell Gate, but Congress was not in a spending mood. In 1850 a public-spirited New York citizen hired French-trained engineer Benjamin Maillefert to remove some of the larger rocks. However, he only succeeded in blowing up the tops of the rocks and ended up killing several men in the process.

On a positive note, it was said that no fishing spot was more popular in the nineteenth century than the rapids of Hell Gate, noted for some of the best striped bass.

The First Obstacle: Hallet's Point Reef

Newton decided that only underwater tunneling would work to clear Hallet's Point reef several yards off the coast of Astoria and a large boulder known as Pot Rock. The reef was to be undermined with a series

63

of passageways charged with explosives and blown up. Congress finally agreed to fund his efforts.

First Newton built a cofferdam, a large watertight enclosure pumped dry to allow underwater work at the water's edge to prevent flooding of the works at high tide. The steam-drilling scow, later renamed the General John Newton in his honor, began its work in 1870. Thirty-seven men were divided into day and night crews that included one engineer, two carpenters, a mechanical draftsman, two divers, drillers, blaster, blacksmith, sailors, firemen, timekeeper, and tide-gauge keeper. The day crew positioned the scow and did the drilling and blasting. The night crew conducted underwater surveys and marked with floats places where additional drilling was needed. For seven years Newton's crew labored, excavating the pit, then inching their way into the solid reef. Tons of rock were blasted from the reef, shoveled into mule carts and hauled to the end of the tunnels to be hoisted to the surface. Once the reef was removed the Hallet's Point channel deepened to twenty-six feet.

While Congress did agree to fund the work, they often delayed payments, which forced the work to be suspended several times. In an 1873 report, Newton wrote, "We have been much delayed and the cost of the operations has been increased by being compelled to work under appropriations not sufficient for rapid and economical progress." According to Newton's own report, the actual work took four years and four months, however, delays caused it to stretch between October 1869 when work began at Hallet's Point Reef until completion in June 1875 (five years and eight months).

When Newton was finally ready to eradicate the reef for good, explosives in 22-inch cartridge cases were placed into 4,427 holes. Newton calculated that dividing the charges would diminish the effect of the explosion beyond the immediate sphere of action.

Naturally, such a landmark undertaking and a years-long construction site was fodder for the press. Most people thought any kind of explosion could cause more harm than good. And because the work took several years and Hell Gate would be a construction site for nearly two decades, with tunnels, workers, cranes and divers, it led to great interest and speculation, as did the Brooklyn Bridge (see chapter 6), another decades-long project occurring during this time.

Newton was well aware of public speculation about the project and had tried to put to rest fears of people who heard there would be a tremendous explosion. He had written to the newspapers, including the *New York Times*, to allay fears, recommending precautions to the public such as opening doors and windows and reducing steam pressure. Some people thought the worst and they would surely all be blown up. Others were more inspired by curiosity and packed the shorelines to watch on the big day. Thousands went to Central Park and more thousands arrived in Astoria to get a close up view. And, there were scores of reporters. A troop of soldiers was sent from West Point to keep people out of harm's way. Everything was cleared from the Hallet's Point cofferdam, but a black and white cat refused to leave. No amount of coaxing would get her to come away with the men.

Anna Newton arrived with their daughter Mary, then four years old, shortly after 2 p.m. Cannon booms began counting down the remaining time before the explosions. At 2:50 Mary stepped up on a box at the firing station on shore and her father guided her hand to the key. She pressed it, sending an immense three-hundred-foot long column of foaming water fifty feet into the air. A spontaneous cheer went up from the thousands watching as the shards of Hallet's Point Reef spattered the waters of Hell Gate and sank.

The *New York Times* (1876) called it a complete scientific success, "A terrific bending force liberated by the finger of a child." The reporter described it as "sharp and not very loud, not in the least of that rending, crushing sound which one is accustomed to connect with nitroglycerine and its relatives." Engineers boarded boats back to Hallet's Point, and three cheers arose from the crowds as Newton passed by on the tug. The crew used scoop nets to gather the dead fish. In the cofferdam, they found the resolute black and white cat unhurt. "She stood on top of one of the boilers mewing piteously," the reporter wrote. (Actually, a few panes of glass did break and some bricks were shaken loose, according to Newton's own report.)

Newton would need an even greater underwater blast for the final obstruction, Flood Rock. Nothing like the underwater blast on the scale that Newton would need had been tried so near the heart of a big city. During the next decade, he led carefully controlled and documented on-the-job experiments and materials. Machinery was invented by the corps for the project. New blasting techniques were developed. Not only was Newton clearing out Hell Gate, he was adding a great deal to the engineering knowledge of the day.

A MAN OF FAITH

After the successful removal of the Hallet's Point reef in 1876, the Xavier Union, the predecessor of the Catholic Club, in which he was active, gave Newton a reception with more than five hundred guests present at their headquarters at 20 West 27th Street in Manhattan. Reform Mayor William Wickham of New York and John Loughlin the first Bishop of Brooklyn attended.

Newton was a devout Catholic, having converted as a young man. Records of the time are sketchy and it is unclear why and when he converted, but it was assumed that when Anna married him, she converted to his religion, largely because there is so little written history about women. Some Internet ancestry sources indicate that some of Anna's ancestors had converted to Catholicism decades before so Newton may have converted when he married her. Whatever the reason, Newton was a devout Catholic and their children were all given Catholic saints names.

According to a notice in a New London newspaper, John and Anna were married in New York by Rev. C.H. Williamson, an Episcopal rector of the French-language Church du St. Sauveur on Duane Street opposite City Hall. However, the only church on that site at the time was St. Charles, a Catholic church. An Episcopal church, however, may have been a compromise as that was the closest Protestant religion to Catholicism.

Meanwhile, Newton and his wife were raising their family and becoming part of the fabric of the city, then still two cities. They lived at 147 Prospect Place between Carlton and Vanderbilt Avenues in the

Prospect Heights section of Brooklyn, along the northern edge of the newly created Prospect Park. Even after Newton and his family years later moved to Manhattan, he continued to attend the Cathedral of St. Joseph in Prospect Heights. Bishop John Hughes, the archbishop of New York, founded this church to serve the large immigrant population of Irish fleeing the famine in their own country, and making New York the largest Irish city in the world.

John and Anna's two surviving sons, Virginius and Augustine, born before they settled in Brooklyn, were soon joined by Victor, Thomas, and Mary, all born in Brooklyn. Another son, Francis, born there, died in infancy. In 1870, when Virginius was 17, Newton requested an appointment for his son at West Point and he is listed in the 1872 roster. In 1880, Virginius was an assistant prefect by the Regents of the University of the State of New York. In 1881, the New York City records, lists him as an engineer's rodman.

Also the year following Hallet's Point Reef, Newton and several of his fellow Catholics along with John McCloskey, archbishop of New York, who was to be named the first American cardinal, planned a trip to the Vatican to visit Pope Pius IX, then known as the Prisoner of the Vatican for refusing to allow the Vatican to be ruled by the newly united Italian government. It was the Golden Episcopal Jubilee. They sailed on the *City of Brussels*, a new steamer that had set the record as the fastest ship afloat. However, a mechanical problem occurred at sea and they had to use the sails.

AN ACTIVE VETERAN

Newton maintained his friendship with Civil War veterans, many of whom, including generals Grant and Sherman, made their home in New York after the Civil War. In 1880 Newton would publicly endorse his friend Winfield Scott Hancock, the Democratic candidate for president, but he was defeated by James A. Garfield. Newton was a member of the Society of the Army of the Potomac and as president in 1884 the fifteenth reunion was held at the Brooklyn Academy of Music, with an audience that filled the entire auditorium and balcony. There was also a gala planned for Coney Island.

Some veterans, like his friend Fitz John Porter, another strong-minded Union general, served in city government. Porter, who was unfairly court-martialed for defying an order he knew would lead to disaster, spent his life fighting against injustice. Porter spent years clearing his name and was vindicated in 1878 and again by General Ulysses Grant in 1888. He served in New York City as police commissioner from 1884 to 1888 and in other high offices.

FLOOD ROCK, THE FINAL OBSTACLE

With nearly all of the obstacles removed from Hell Gate, all that remained was Flood Rock, a nine-acre obstacle south of Wards Island. Only 230 square feet of this behemoth showed above the water. However, when work began here in 1876, it was once again shut down for lack of funding, during a depression, and three years lapsed before work could begin again. This time Newton insisted on some amenities for his crew, such as a staircase in one of the shafts to replace an elevator hoisted by a rope. Also, the army purchased a whaleboat to provide ferry service for the crew. Earlier workmen were expected to get to work on their own and were usually overcharged by local boat owners. He also called for a drying room inside the excavation to workers could dry their clothes and warm up near fires before heading home. And he insisted the mules have a warmed stable where they could rest.

A seawall was built around this area and inside this enclosure, a large lift tower was built over the main shaft site and drilling began. A seventy-foot shaft was sunk and in the other, a stairway led to these tunnels. For nine years, Newton's crew excavated material that was hauled up by mules and men. Teams of mules were used in the tunnels to draw wagonloads of rock away. Years later, the *New York Times* ran an obituary for "Old Dan," one of the mules who "served Uncle Sam for over 30 years, nine of which were in the tunnel under Hell Gate." Old Dan was nearly forty years old and having become crippled, had to be put to rest.

Newton left nothing to chance. He wanted the Flood Rock explosion documented for the sake of scientific research and also to protect himself and the corps against any fraudulent charges of damage. By now, he was accustomed to erroneous information appearing in the press, complaints, and even lawsuits, such as a case against his steam drilling machine, which someone claimed was not Newton's original design. Many newspapers published the disparaging statements made by those claiming to have invented it. Newton waited it out patiently, and was vindicated by the courts. "General Newton's Position Sustained—A Claim Against the Federal Government Knocked on the Head," reported the *Brooklyn Daily Eagle.*

Newton was a remarkably patient man and knew how to use the press to his advantage; he wanted the public to be informed about what was going on, so that rumor and speculation did not prevail. As it was, there was considerable complaining about the "works" and how they affected the communities.

Before the final blast for Flood Rock, Newton had his officers organize a party of observers that fanned out for miles to measure, on crude instruments, the effect of the blast in their area and other pertinent information. Parties of two officers and six enlisted men proceeded by rail and horseback to points as far away as Massachusetts and Rhode Island to measure any shock waves.

On October 10, 1885, everything was set to go. "It was a drab Sunday," wrote Rust, "which added to the fears of residents who were saying it would be the end of the world." At 9 a.m. one of the engineers went to the bombproof shelter to supervise the filling of the storage battery with 150 gallons of "Electropaian fluid," the magic mixture to activate the many battery cells.

Once everything was set up at noon, Newton arrived, and walked through the crowds of spectators already gathered at the site to join the engineers and workmen at the shelter were they were preparing to activate the batteries. He then boarded a white launch for inspection tour, first to the drill scow, where a six-pound cannon was ready to signal the event. The entire nine acres of Flood Rock, 1,200 feet by 602 feet, was studded with explosives, what they called "rack a rock," made of chlorate of potash and dinitrobenzole. They used 250,000 pounds of dynamite. Then he picked up Anna and Mary and went to the firing station behind the shelter at Hallet's Point.

The rain stopped at one o'clock and the Manhattan shore was lined with spectators. Some enterprising entrepreneurs had sold one-dollar "seats" for the occasion, which obviously meant permission to sit on the ground. The patients on Ward's Island, a hospital for the mentally ill (then called an insane asylum), were allowed outdoors, although the prisoners on Blackwell's Island, now known as Roosevelt Island, remained in their cells. At 2:30 a gun was fired to signal the guard boats to close off the entrances to Hell Gate. The charged mine below was flooded to prevent excessive scattering of rocks. At 2:40 the second gun was fired for those who wished to take cover.

Finally, Mary, now twelve, at a nod from her father, pressed the key that simultaneously set off the charge. It was estimated that fifty thousand spectators and one hundred cameras on the shores of the East River witnessed the event. As Rust described it: "With a muffled rumble from the depths of Hell Gate, nine acres of the river was lifted into the air, a tremendous mass of rock and foam 150 feet high. A sickening jar was felt on land, and seconds later waves lapped the shores. The greatest single explosion ever produced by man was over." (There would never be a manmade explosion this large until the atomic bomb sixty years later.)

Engineering News and American Contract Journal gave glowing praise to Newton. "Although the volume of explosives here used exceeded sixfold the greatest charge ever previously fired in the world, the work of the engineers was so well done and the precautionary measures of General Newton so well taken, that no accident or delay of any kind occurred." The *New York Times* devoted their entire front page to the event and newspapers all over the world from Chicago to Australia reported on the explosion of the nine-acre boulder.

Ships and boats, including petroleum barges, which had never before been allowed through Hell Gate, were now able to navigate this passage easily. Shipping trade increased to some $4 million worth of cargo a day, justifying the millions of dollars for the un-snagging operation. A new life was infused into the Port of New York, which was once again able to assert itself as the undisputed leading port in the nation at the time.

To this day the US Army Corps of Engineers continues its mission of maintaining depths of federal navigation channels in New York harbor.

Leaving the Army for Public Office

New York mayor William Russell Grace wanted someone honest to head up the Department of Public Works and asked General Newton to take on the job now that his work was done at Hell Gate. Grace, born in Ireland in 1832, had come to America with little but his intelligence and ambition and eventually founded W.R. Grace Steamship Company. While he had never taken a serious interest in politics, he was reform-minded and wanted to rid the city of corruption so entrenched in Tammany Hall.

Newton would replace the previous commissioner, Rollin Squire, who had been forced out by scandal, but since the city's very first commissioner of public works was the infamous Boss William Marcy Tweed himself, it was a department entrenched in graft and scandal. Building public works meant giving out contracts, and that had always been a problem. *Harper's Weekly* featured a cartoon by the famous political artist Thomas Nast showing Squire fired and Newton hired.

The *New York Times* on August 28, 1886, reported on a comment from the *Army and Navy Journal*: "We believe that the appointment of Gen. Newton will be followed by such a complete deliverance of his department from political associations that the intrigues will find no foothold here. Upon this the success of his administration depends."

Newton had many ideas on ways to improve the city's transportation and other services. However, despite his desire to make things better, he was not used to dealing with the kinds of corruption and intrigue involved in getting things done in city government. He was accustomed to working with his engineers, who were focused on completing their task as safely as possible, which was facilitated by a clear chain of command. It is doubtful that Newton could stomach the type of intrigue that was so entrenched in Tammany Hall politics. Less than two years later, he refused reappointment to the post and on April 2, 1888, accepted the presidency of the Panama Railroad Company, headquartered in New York, a job he kept until his death seven years later.

Newton had been awarded the degree of LL.D. by St. Francis Xavier College in 1886; he was a member of the National Academy of Sciences, and an honorary member of the American Society of Civil Engineers.

BURIAL AT WEST POINT

On May 5, 1895, John Newton died from chronic rheumatism and pneumonia at his home at 40 West 57th Street, where he had lived for many years. He was seventy-three. Four companies of the First Artillery from Governors Island and Fort Hamilton acted as an infantry escort in a procession from 75th Street and Fifth Avenue to St. Francis Xavier's Church on 16th Street between Fifth and Sixth Avenues.

Among his pallbearers was Fitz John Porter, Col. George Gillespie, another Southerner who remained loyal to the Union, and like Newton, graduated second in his class at West Point in 1841. He received the Medal of Honor for carrying messages through enemy lines.

The officers and employees of the Panama Railroad, representatives from the Southern Society, Lt. General George W. Smith, late of the Confederate Army, George Francis Train, Lt. Loyal Farragut, and other military officers. Lt. Farragut, son of the famous admiral, was a cousin of Fitz John Porter. Miss Betty Newton was most likely his niece, Washington Irving Newton's daughter.

Anna and their children followed the casket. High mass was said by Father Prendergast, who noted, "General Newton united all the noble qualifies of a soldier and patriot with the humility and zeal of the Christian." He is buried at West Point and, like Abraham Lincoln, Newton had his infant son Francis who died in 1873 buried with him.

Six months after Newton's death, his son Augustine, thirty-eight, died of an apparent overdose of a medication often used to "brace up from overwork." He had been a partner of J.A. Rodgers, contractors who were constructing the wide Harlem River Driveway along the edge of the Harlem River for the city's wealthy to race their horse carriages. He was married to Charlotte Wilkin and they had a two-year-old daughter.

Anna lived to be eighty-eight and died of pneumonia June 28, 1914, in their Manhattan apartment. She was buried beside her husband at West Point.

In 1899 the Corps of Engineers named a 175-foot paddle wheeler in Newton's honor. It was used as a maritime courthouse and visited by several presidents and in 1958, engineers sold it to the University of

Minnesota to use as showboat. It lasted one hundred years as a showboat until it was destroyed by fire in 2000.

In 1901, Cyrus B. Comstock delivered an address about Newton before the National Academy, praising his work. Comstock, also in the corps of engineers, was General Grant's senior aide-de-camp.

In 1936, the Triborough Bridge (now the Robert F. Kennedy Bridge) was erected to span the three boroughs that come together at Hell Gate. This three-part bridge complex has also become a National Civil Engineering Landmark. First, a suspension bridge crosses Hell Gate from Queens to Ward's Island. From there a truss bridge crosses into the Bronx, and another crosses into Manhattan.

From the bridge today, it's hard to imagine all the chaos that went on in the waters below. Of course, there is much less traffic through the passage now that most of the harbor's commerce is centered in Port Elizabeth and Port Newark, on the western side of the harbor. Hell Gate today is a passage for pleasure craft.

The bass fishing is said to be quite good.

6

Emily Warren Roebling
and The Great Bridge

*I am still feeling well enough to stoutly maintain against all critics
(including my only son) that I have more brains, common sense, and
know-how generally than any two engineers civil or uncivil that I
have ever met, and but for me the Brooklyn Bridge would never have
had the name of Roebling in any way connected with it! It would
have been Kingsley's Bridge if it had ever been built! Your father was
for years dead to all interest in that work.*
—Emily Warren Roebling in a letter to her son, 1898

This is the story of an exceptional woman who spent eleven
years carrying out her disabled husband's role as chief engineer until
the Brooklyn Bridge was completed in 1883. She handled day-to-day
supervision and project management at the construction site. She dealt
with the bridge trustees, politicians, the press, competing engineers, and
the workers. In 1881, two years before completion, she led the trustees
across a five-foot-wide plank walkway over the East River between the
two cities. When they reached the Manhattan side, the trustees, several
clearly nervous on this "walk," gave a champagne toast to the bridge and
to Emily Roebling.

By the time the bridge was finished, Emily, now forty, had become
the public face of the era's most massive engineering and construction

project involving six hundred workers and costing $3.2 million, to be forever known as the Eighth Wonder of the World, and depicted in art and photography more than any other structure in the world for decades to come.

Nevertheless, the extent of Emily's work on the Brooklyn Bridge was never officially recognized except for thanking her for being a loyal helpmate to her ailing husband. It wasn't until the centennial of the bridge that she was finally discovered, or rediscovered, for her role. Today she is granted co-star credits with her engineer husband, Washington Roebling.

AN UNUSUAL EDUCATION FOR A WOMAN

Emily was born in 1843 in Cold Spring, Putnam County, New York, one of eleven children of Sylvanus Warren, a New York State assemblyman, and Phoebe Lickley Warren. Emily's brother Gouverneur Kemble Warren, known as GK, a West Point graduate and thirteen years her senior, paid for his favorite little sister, then fifteen years old, to attend secondary school, not something most young women did at the time. Emily became a student at Georgetown Visitation Convent in Washington, DC, which still exists today. Along with the traditional female pursuits such as housekeeping, weaving, and piano, Emily's curriculum included numerous courses in science and algebra, history, geography, and French. She graduated with highest honors in 1860 and returned to Cold Spring to live with her recently widowed mother, whose health was failing.

Four years later, during the Civil War, Emily convinced her family to let her visit GK, now a general in the Union Army stationed in Virginia. There Emily met Washington Roebling, an engineer on her brother's staff. It was love at first sight for the couple and after a long distance courtship of many letters (only his survive), they were married in Cold Spring in 1865. The newlyweds moved to Cincinnati, Ohio, where the groom assisted his father, John Roebling, with the construction of what would be at the time the world's longest steel suspension bridge over the Ohio River between that city and Covington, Kentucky, and which one hundred years later, would be named for him.

John Roebling greatly admired his new daughter-in-law and in 1867 he sent the couple to Europe, where Washington studied caissons

Emily Warren Roebling

in preparation for what was originally to be called the Great Bridge between Brooklyn and Manhattan. Emily, who already had an interest in engineering, visited many of the sites with her husband. While staying with family members at the Roebling ancestral home in Muhlhausen, then part of Prussia, Emily gave birth to their son John A. Roebling II in 1867. On their return to the United States in 1869, they moved into a Brooklyn Heights brownstone home, where the construction of the bridge was getting under way.

Washington and Emily and their toddler son lived at 110 Columbia Heights, at this time the posh part of what was then a separate city from Manhattan. The backs of the brownstone homes on Columbia Heights faced the harbor, with two-level yards and gardens for enjoying the view, sometimes with stairways between the two levels. (This landscape was later destroyed by the Brooklyn-Queens Expressway.) Brooklyn Heights at the time was the unchallenged social, cultural, and moral center of Brooklyn life. Each Sunday, people came from Manhattan on the always-crowded "Beecher Boats" to sit in Plymouth Church, on Orange Street, and listen to the famous preacher Henry Ward Beecher.

THE DESPERATE NEED FOR THE GREAT BRIDGE

The congestion of hundreds of ferries crossing the East River carrying passengers between Brooklyn and their jobs in New York had become dangerous, and during freezing or foggy conditions, passage was near impossible. While a very large city on its own, Brooklyn wanted to bridge the gap, so to speak, in its status as "second" to the city across the river. This was the Gilded Age, an era when rich men were crisscrossing the country with railroads, so in 1867, the former politician Henry Murphy, owner of the *Brooklyn Eagle,* a widely circulated daily newspaper, once edited by Walt Whitman, brought together thirty-eight men to form a corporation that would build a span across the East River to carry trains as well as wagons and pedestrians. The New York Bridge Company was so named because it was to be a bridge *to* that location. They sold stock to raise the millions needed and sought to obtain the federal approval that the state government said they needed.

William Kingsley, a wealthy contractor from Brooklyn with ties to
Hugh McLaughlin, that city's equivalent to New York's corrupt Tammany Hall boss William Marcy Tweed, agreed to fund the project. So the
two cities' "bosses" became forces in getting the bridge built—for a price,
of course. A later investigation found that Kingsley's pay as a contractor
was suspiciously high and that he had profited unfairly. Regardless, the
trustees and the bosses wanted the best engineer they could find. John A.
Roebling was already well known for his bridges at Niagara, Pittsburgh,
and Cincinnati. Based on his past success, the company actually hired
him before he had submitted any formal plans for the bridge.

Roebling organized what was later known as the "bridge party," a sort
of scouting group that included hand-picked engineers he knew to give
an assessment to Congress, which had to approve the bridge as a legal
post road, that is, a road over which mail could be transported. One of
these was General John Newton, of the Army Corps of Engineers, who
was in charge of New York harbor defenses at this time, and would later
become famous himself for removing boulders and other obstacles from
Hell Gate (see chapter 5). The engineers, along with Kingsley and some
Brooklyn businessmen and politicians, traveled by train to visit Roebling's other works, and final approval for Roebling's design came from
Congress in June 1869.

In addition to it being the longest and most expensive bridge ever
built in the world, the Great Bridge was to be the first steel-*wire* suspension bridge ever constructed. In this type of suspension system, wire
is spun into strands and bound together into cables. Unfortunately, John
Roebling did not live to see his masterpiece completed. In 1869, before
construction began, Emily's father-in-law, while doing a survey with
Washington at his side, got his foot crushed when it was caught between
the dock and a ferryboat. His toes had to be amputated, but he refused
proper treatment, preferring his own homeopathic remedies. As a result,
he developed tetanus and died several weeks later.

Washington took over as chief engineer. He had designed and was
building pneumatic caissons, air-tight enclosed chambers like elevator
shafts, to allow workers to dig out foundations at great depths using
compressed air to keep water and mud out of their way. Washington had

learned about this construction technique while in Europe and probably knew more about it than any engineer in America. The Brooklyn shaft was established without too many problems, but on the Manhattan side, the river bed was much deeper, so workers were exposed to the compressed air for longer periods.

While working on the Manhattan tower, Washington suffered several attacks of caisson's disease, or the bends, which causes muscular paralysis and sometimes death because of nitrogen bubbles caught in the bloodstream when the body is subject to high pressure. The condition also wreaked havoc on the nervous system. An average of one hundred men a week quit working in the caissons. At the time nobody knew anything about how to treat or cure the disease. In 1872 Washington had his most acute attack and this time did not recover. He and Emily traveled to Germany so that he could get treatment, but it proved ineffective and the couple returned. Washington was partially paralyzed, nearly blind, and bedridden. Unable to go to the construction site, he relied on Emily to see that the bridge got built.

As Washington himself said later, Emily was quite literally "his eyes, his legs, his good right arm."

A WOMAN AS BOSS

Not only was Emily well educated, she was truly interested in science and engineering and had already learned a great deal about it, from her husband, her father-in-law, and while visiting those sites in Europe. She had a retentive mind, a natural gift for mathematics, and began to study the strength of materials, wire cable construction, stress analysis, and physics. She was a quick study, a determined advocate for the bridge, and a woman who loved her husband and family.

Emily was also a woman of passion and determination, and those who knew her realized how remarkable she was. Nevertheless, this was an era when it was inconceivable to think that a woman was capable of such an undertaking. A woman could certainly be an angel of mercy, ministering to her ill husband in the sickroom and carrying his messages to his workers, while he allegedly watched and supervised through his telescope from his window facing the harbor and the bridge construction.

This was the myth that survived over the years. In fact, there was an illustration made of this image decades later by Vincent A. Svoboda, which appeared in many newspapers and magazines over the years. It depicts the engineer sitting up in his bed with the telescope aimed at the bridge. On the bed beside him are blueprints, drawings, rulers, and other engineering instruments.

As David McCullough pointed out in *The Great Bridge*, "Since every piece of written communication from the house on Columbia Heights to the bridge offices was in her hand, there was, understandably, a strong suspicion that she was doing more than merely taking down what her husband dictated. At first she was credited only with brushing up his English, which may have been the case. But by and by it was common gossip that hers was the real mind behind the great work and that this most important monumental engineering triumph of the age was actually the doing of a woman, which as the general proposition was taken in some quarters to be both preposterous and calamitous. In truth, by then she had a thorough grasp of the engineering involved." One day a manufacturer came to the house to find out how a particular part of the superstructure should be formed. Emily made a drawing to show him how it could be done, explaining each step carefully. Whatever doubts there may have been among the bridge people, about Emily's ability to make decisions and judgments on the work, was long gone.

Emily went to the bridge regularly, sometimes two or three times a day. She could speak as well as her husband on bridge matters and no one on the engineering staff ever hesitated to accept her word. Some of the younger engineers, who had never met Washington in person, believed him to be mentally incapacitated and Emily—a woman—to be running the show.

And the more Emily did, the more the gossips talked.

In addition to keeping records, answering mail, recording correspondence, and instructing the field engineers, she was able to conduct negotiations with companies seeking contracts for materials and she was liaison with the bridge trustees. Emily kept her own records as well, such as scrapbooks of all of the ephemera, including newspaper articles, letters, and photos. Much of this material is in the archives of the Alexander Library at Rutgers University in New Brunswick, New Jersey.

THE MAYOR OF BROOKLYN WANTS ROEBLING FIRED

In 1882, a year before the bridge would be completed, Emily and Washington and their son, now fifteen, went to Newport, Rhode Island, to visit her brother GK who had been stationed there and was suffering what would be his final and fatal illness. Gouverneur Warren, who graduated second in his class at West Point, was a hero of the Battle of Little Round Top at Gettysburg. In a later battle he somehow infuriated General Phil Sheridan, who unfairly relieved him of his command. Warren spent the rest of his life trying to clear his name. That pardon was finally granted by President Rutherford Hayes, but Warren would never know about it. He suffered from several physical ailments, including diabetes, which led to liver disease, the official cause of death at fifty-two. However, many said he died of a broken heart. Memorial statues of Warren were later established at Little Round Top and also at Grand Army Plaza in Brooklyn.

While the Roeblings were away, some of the new and younger bridge company trustees, who had little knowledge of bridge building but needed to impress their constituents—led an attempt to fire Washington because of construction delays. Brooklyn mayor Seth Low, one of the trustees who had never seen the chief engineer, claimed he was convinced "that at every point there is a weakness in the management of the Brooklyn Bridge. The engineering part of the structure—the most important—is in the hands of a sick man." In reality, the problems were caused by contractors and politicians trying to profit from the use of substandard equipment, causing delays and overruns. (Murphy, Kingsley, and James Stranahan, also a trustee and former president of the Brooklyn Parks Commission, were later blamed.)

"Had Mr. Roebling done his duty rather than becoming the cat's paw of the bridge ring, he might have saved millions of dollars," Low claimed. When he learned that Roebling was *vacationing* in Newport with his family, the irate mayor chased them down and confronted Roebling there. Low told Roebling it was time to step aside. He could remain consulting engineer but C.C. Martin, who served as the first assistant engineer, would be made chief engineer. Low suggested this was a perfectly honorable move and history would still remember him as the builder.

Roebling refused and told Lowe he would have to fire him. Low stormed off vowing to do just that. Fortunately for Washington Roebling, his wife had a more sensible way to deal with the mayor's threat and her husband's inability to finesse the situation. While mourning the death of her brother, Emily used her political savvy to make sure her husband was not fired. She sought out the board's controller Ludwig Semler, a man she believed would stand up for her husband. "Mr. R is very anxious for me to go to Brooklyn to convey to you a few messages from him," she wrote. "Can you see me at your home or office?" Emily asked. "There are some few old friends in the trustees who know him well and who have always stood by him." She represented and defended her husband before the board. After Emily's plea, the trustees voted ten to seven in Roebling's favor with Semler and some of the others strongly defending Roebling and overruling the mayor. Emily wrote this to Semler: "Thank you for your generous defense of Mr. Roebling at the last meeting of the board of trustees." Roebling remained as chief engineer, thanks to the actual chief engineer. Nevertheless, Emily would despise Seth Low for the rest of her life.

THE PEOPLE'S BRIDGE OPENS

Finally, after fourteen years, six hundred workers, and $15 million (320 million in twenty-first-century money), the bridge was ready to be used. A few days before the official opening, it was agreed that Emily should be the first to ride over the bridge in a carriage along with her son, carrying a live rooster in her lap as a symbol of progress and prosperity. From one end of the bridge to the other, the men had stopped their work to cheer and lift their hats as she passed by.

The opening on May 24, 1883, was to be the biggest celebration in New York since the opening of the Erie Canal in 1825 and would be known as the "People's Day." Mayor Low proclaimed it an official holiday in Brooklyn. Vendors hawked flags, gumdrops, pictures of John and Washington Roebling, bridge buttons, and more. The mayor planned a party for President Chester Arthur, who was from New York.

Meanwhile, because her husband would not be able to participate in the day Seth Low was planning, Emily would bring everyone to him.

In addition to her skills as an engineer, Emily had the perspective of a first-rate public relations executive and made sure her husband would get his due credit. She organized a reception at their home for the trustees, the mayors, the governor, and president. She drew up a guest list and designed the invitation. Emily also commissioned an oil painting of her husband, and filled the house with flowers.

John Kingsley escorted the New York delegation including President Arthur and Governor Grover Cleveland, who had once been the mayor of New York, across the span on the elevated promenade to meet the Brooklyn contingent led by Mayor Low at the opposite tower. In all the speeches made atop the bridge, only that of New York Congressman Abram Hewitt recognized Emily's contribution to the bridge as a woman in this day and age being truly able to use her education, yet softening it with the usual Victorian sentiment about feminine modesty. "It is thus an everlasting monument to *the self-sacrificing devotion of woman*, and of her capacity for that higher education from which she has been too long disbarred. The name of Mrs. Emily Warren Roebling will thus be inseparably associated with all that is admirable in human nature, and with all this is wonderful in the constructive world of art."

The Brooklyn Bridge opened to rave reviews, of course. It was the highest structure in New York—only the Trinity Church steeple on Wall Street was higher—and it was designed by a man who loved to walk. John Roebling designed the special promenade meant only for pedestrians eighteen feet above the then cable car and horse cart traffic. His bridge over the Ohio River had a pedestrian walkway, too, but not as grandly planned out as this one. More than 150,000 people a day paid a toll of a penny in 1883 to be above it all, to take a brisk walk of just over a mile. People were suddenly able to walk out over a river, higher than they had ever been in their lives to look out over both cities and their magnificent harbor.

To this day a walk across the bridge is a moving experience. The bridge itself is alive and moving, as much as seven feet up and down at the center. Each cable contains 3,515 miles of wire wrapped in an outer skin of soft wire, much the way the bass strings of a piano are made. Suspenders hang like harp strings from the cables down to the bridge floor and diagonal stays radiate across these, forming a beautiful pattern. It's a bit like walking between two giant harps, or gossamer spider webs. Two of the four cables that suspend the bridge, each more than fifteen inches in diameter, enclose the promenade. You can feel them vibrate when you put your hand on them. The great Gothic arches that support the cable continue to this day to inspire photographers and artists. As Mayor Seth Low said at the dedication, "No one who has ever been upon it can ever forget it."

SOME FAINT PRAISE FOR EMILY

Most of the people involved in creating the bridge realized that Emily was the one who got it built. Even the press knew, but hesitated to state clearly just what her role had been, for it was so far outside of society's ingrained notions of womanhood. The *Brooklyn Eagle* described Emily's role in a way that fit the prescribed notions of female behavior of the time: modest, marginal, and mostly silent. "The true woman possesses, above all attributes, that loveliest and most womanly characteristic—modesty. Out of deference to Mrs. Roebling's aversion to posing in public and standing apart from her sex, those who have long been aware of her noble devotion and the incalculable services she rendered to the people of the two cities, to the world indeed, have discreetly kept their knowledge to themselves."

The *Eagle* also gave Emily the role of communicator. "Day after day, when she could be spared from the sickroom, in cold and wet, the devoted wife exchanged the duties of chief nurse for those of chief engineer of the bridge, explaining knotty points, examining results for herself, and thus, she established the most perfect means of communication between the structure and its author. How well she discharged this self-imposed duty the grand and beautiful causeway best tells."

The *New York World*, published by Joseph Pulitzer, carried a short homage to Emily the next day, the only one that omits the flowery language and gets to the truth. "A gentleman of this city well acquainted with the family said that as soon as Mr. Roebling was stricken with that peculiar fever which has since prostrated him, Mrs. Roebling applied herself to the study of engineering, and she succeeded so well that in a short time she was able to assume the duties of chief engineer."

As reported in a 1996 article in the *Journal of the Association of Collegiate Schools of Architecture*: "Among all the huzzahs for the bridge, some reporters recognized Emily, without ruining her reputation as a woman when it was unseemly for women to do 'man's work.' Emily's presence as a woman in the development of suspension bridge technology was threatening to the public. Her appearances, however, as a wife in the service of her husband, selfless and tireless, or as a goddess arriving effortlessly to apply herself to the task, carried on for another century."

GOING FORWARD IN A MALE WORLD

The Roeblings left Brooklyn to move upstate to Troy while their son attended Rensselaer Polytechnic Institute, Washington's alma mater. Earlier John had attended the Collegiate School in New York and Brooklyn Boys' Prep. Washington would never fully recover from caisson's disease, although it became less debilitating and his health gradually improved enough so he was able to get around and lead a fairly normal life, although he tired easily. With his two brothers, Washington was a shareholder of the Roebling Sons Company, which had become the world's leading producer of wire rope, so he was well enough off not to need to work at the plant.

Emily, however, was not about to let her engineering skills go to waste, and she supervised the construction of a large and comfortable new home complete with bowling alley, a sport she enjoyed. She installed a stuffed rooster on the drawing room mantel to represent her experience with the Brooklyn Bridge. There was a dog named Ponto, whom Emily was very attached to, completing the family. (Her husband also kept a pet water snake, which she was not crazy about.) By this time their son John had married and moved away from New Jersey, eventually settling in Florida.

However, Emily did not "settle down" into a conventional married woman's role. And how could she after what she had just accomplished? She was more than a well-off society woman doing her duty with works of charity. She had long been involved with the Daughters of the American Revolution, but that was because of her family heritage, and certainly was not enough to satisfy her intellectually and emotionally. She later wrote two books about her family's early American roots, *Richard Warren of the Mayflower and Some of his Descendants,* published in 1901, and the *Journal of Silas Constant,* published just after her death.

More relevant to Emily, long a suffragist and proponent of equality for women, was her active involvement in Sorosis, the nation's first professional and literary club for women. Sorosis was founded in 1868 as a result of women journalists being denied tickets to the New York Press Club event honoring Charles Dickens's first visit to the United States. The male organizers claimed that the presence of the women would make the occasion "promiscuous." This so offended the women, that they founded their own club, calling it Sorosis, a botanical term referring to plants with a grouping of flowers that bore fruit. It was meant to symbolize women's determination to transform supposedly delicate and feeble ladies into important members of public society. They championed women's issues such as pressuring Columbia College to allow women students.

Formed the same year as Boston's New England Woman's Club, they inspired the formation of such clubs across the country because at the time there were no women's clubs of any kind, not even church groups, bridge, or garden clubs. One Sorosis gathering asked: Do business pursuits improve women mentally, morally, socially, and physically? In a letter to her son, Emily wrote, "Those on the affirmative side of the question comfortably annihilated the unfortunates who had the negative."

The forward-thinking owners of Delmonico's restaurant in New York allowed the Sorosis women to rent a private room at the restaurant, although at the time, women were not allowed to dine there unaccompanied. (Delmonico's would later become the first restaurant to allow women to dine unescorted.)

Emily was also secretary treasurer of the New Jersey Board of Lady Managers for the Columbian Exposition in Chicago in 1893, one of her most gratifying undertakings. She was at the dedication of the exposition's New Jersey building. While there with her husband, a French duchess referring to the Brooklyn Bridge complimented her skill as an engineer.

Emily traveled frequently on her own and in 1896 attended the coronation of Czar Nicholas II in Moscow, where she was presented in court.

Back home, she gave some illustrated lectures on the event. Emily also chaired the committee on statistics for the New Jersey Board, gathering data on women employed outside the home, types of work, and number of patents obtained by woman. She was also president of the board of trustees of Evelyn College, a short-lived institution for women associated with Princeton.

In 1899 at the age of fifty-six, after a two-year course, Emily graduated from law school at New York University at a ceremony at the original Madison Square Garden and won the fifty-dollar first prize for her essay, "A Wife's Disabilities," which she read to a "stunned" audience. She proposed eliminating laws discriminating against wives and widows. "Married women are the equivalent of idiots and slaves," she wrote, "and property should belong to both partners equally." This was at a time when her husband was pulling in millions from his share of Roebling Steel Works. And while her husband provided a comfortable life, none of it belonged to her. Any money she earned from her speaking engagements and other activities would have belonged to Washington. Think what she might have done to advance the cause of women with some capital of her own. Her essay was printed in its entirety in the *Albany Law Journal* in 1899. All daily newspapers in New York and Trenton carried an article about the graduates and Emily's prize but few said much about the subject of the paper.

New York reform mayor William Lafayette Strong held a tea for Emily and the other graduates. While the *New York Times* did report on the graduation, it listed all the women with their husbands' names, in her case Mrs. Washington Roebling. Not a mention of "Emily." Washington attended the graduation but responded to a reporter inquiring about his wife's prize-winning essay, "I never heard her essay until tonight and I do not agree with one word she has said."

Three years later, on February 28, 1903, Emily died of stomach cancer at fifty-nine and was buried in Cold Spring. Although Washington never fully recovered from caisson's disease, he remarried and lived to be eighty-nine. He died in 1926 and is buried with Emily in Cold Spring.

A Century Passes Before Her Work Is Recognized

While Emily Roebling always considered the Brooklyn Bridge her proudest achievement, during the entire decade of her work there was virtually no attempt, other than gossip, to make the public aware of her importance in the completion of such a project. At the time, women were not considered capable of such work, and in their role as their husbands' helpmates, modesty prevented them from bragging or taking credit. At the time it would actually appear offensive to have a woman identified as playing a man's role. Emily Warren Roebling was too smart and refined to openly complain about not being recognized in the press. Fortunately for us, her son saved her letters, where she was more open with her feelings. They are on file at the Alexander Library, Rutgers University archives.

Even into the twentieth century, efforts to efface Emily's work from history continued. At the fiftieth anniversary of the bridge in 1933, an article in the *New York Times* focused only on the men involved in its construction.

In 1950, funds were raised by public subscription to create a plaque for the Brooklyn Bridge that would include Emily's name. Nevertheless, it reads like something expressed in the previous century and makes any self-respecting woman cringe. "Back of every great work we can find the self-sacrificing devotion of a woman." It continues, "With faith and courage, she helped her stricken husband Col. Washington A. Roebling, C.E., 1837–1926 to complete the construction of this bridge from the plans of his father John A. Roebling, C.E. 1806–1869, who gave his life to the bridge."

In 1953 for the seventieth anniversary, the *New York Times* reported that Washington Roebling supervised the work from his room for eleven years, watching the construction with field glasses, and using his wife as an intermediary. Had they done some fact-checking, they would have known that Roebling, by his own admission, could not see much of anything from his window because of his disease. Again, the image of that Svoboda drawing pops up in stories about the bridge.

It wasn't until the hundredth anniversary of the bridge in 1983 that the truth began to come out. Feminism was advancing once again and newspapers were beginning to realize that women and what they did might be newsworthy. There were also many more women journalists by this time and more research about the bridge was called for. David McCullough in his 1972 book, *The Great Bridge*, devoted a chapter to Emily's role, but held back the full credit she deserved. In 1983, Professor Marilyn Weigold, of Pace University, who may have been the first to actually investigate the archives at Rutgers from a new perspective and read the scores of letters Emily wrote to her son, published a small academic book, *Silent Builder: Emily Warren Roebling and the Brooklyn Bridge*.

Since 1982, the Association of Professional Women in Construction has bestowed an Emily Roebling award. The national Women's Hall of Fame in 1983 (centennial year) created an "Emily" award for excellence in the area of business, science, or technology. The Roebling Museum in New Jersey has an Emily Roebling STEAM Day Camp (science, technology, engineering, arts, and math) to encourage children to discover engineering.

Five years before she died, Emily told her son that the Brooklyn Bridge was her crowning achievement. Were it not for her son saving her letters, we would not have any idea about her inner feelings.

John Wolfe Ambrose:
Bringing in the Biggest Ships

With no personal concern in the improvements outside of what is felt by every member of the commercial organization of New York, he worked patiently for nine years to bring about these improvements, and at last sees the beginning of the work which shall make this the finest harbor in the world . . . a man whose crowning achievement was that he had procured for the port of New York an entrance channel 2,000 feet wide and 40 feet deep from the Narrows to the ocean!
—Governor Theodore Roosevelt, April 26, 1899

Like a true Renaissance man, John Ambrose had many interests and talents. His son-in-law George F. Shrady Jr. said his "giant intellect, coupled with his remarkable executive ability and constructive genius, conceived plans for public improvements so vast and comprehensive that he occupied a unique position among men in that he was far ahead of his time. He was one of our most public spirited citizens, to whom New York owes an eternal debt of gratitude." Shrady further described Ambrose as "a man of commanding presence" who possessed "a keen sense of humor, and was by nature genial and kindly."

Over six feet tall and well tailored, Ambrose wore very prominent sideburns, or burnsides, a fashion begun during the Civil War by General

Ambrose Burnside (no relation). A variation on jowl muttonchops, they connect thick sideburns by way of a mustache and leave the chin clean.

Ambrose accomplished a great deal for the city in his lifetime. He built the Second Avenue elevated subway, laid ninety miles of gas mains in ninety days, designed the city's street-cleaning program, developed the South Brooklyn waterfront for shipping, operated a ferry company between there and lower Manhattan, and built an amusement park that saw the likes of Buffalo Bill and Annie Oakley. But his tireless efforts for nine years to get a recalcitrant Congress to appropriate funds to build the deep shipping channel that kept New York harbor a world port by the beginning of the twentieth century is his most lasting gift.

AN IRISH IMMIGRANT

John Wolfe Ambrose was born January 10, 1838, at Newcastle, Limerick County, an area of southern Ireland known for dairy farming and produce such as barley and oats, and where Protestants and Catholics lived together peacefully. It is in a bowl shaped valley on the River Ara, which flows into the River Deel. Ambrose was twelve or fourteen when he came to New York with his parents and possibly other family members, but little is known about his early life or his parents. Records from Castle Garden, the former Castle Clinton then serving as an immigration center, show only one Ambrose family during this time, a twelve-year-old John Ambrose arriving in August 1851 along with his mother Bridget and sisters Johanna, sixteen, and Bridget, eleven. The father, also named John, forty, had arrived three months earlier. While it is not certain this is the same Ambrose family, the age matches what we know about John Wolfe Ambrose.

A cousin, Daniel, five years younger than Ambrose, came to New York in 1865 and became a prominent physician in Brooklyn Heights. Another physician cousin, J.K. Ambrose, became the Staten Island coroner. According to Arthur Ambrose, a descendant of Daniel speaking in 2003, the earliest Ambrose ancestors were farmers, but there were many doctors and ministers in the family in Ireland.

Ambrose himself had planned to become a Presbyterian minister and worked so that he could attend Princeton University, then known as the

Replica of the original bust of John Wolfe Ambrose, which will be installed in a new monument at the Battery in the near future.

Princeton Theological School, which was founded by Presbyterians, primarily the Scotch Irish. He left after a year to attend New York University, then known as University of the City of New York, where he found a mentor and lifetime friend in Dr. Howard Crosby, a Greek scholar with whom Ambrose enjoyed reading the classics—in Greek—for many years. In addition to the classics of Greek and Latin, the curriculum at that time included algebra, geometry, trigonometry and surveying, calculus, and analytical geometry. (Crosby, a Presbyterian minister, was chancellor of New York University from 1870 to 1881, the first one to allow women to attend classes. He died in 1891.)

In 1862 after his studies at New York University, Ambrose, who was focused on public service, took a newspaper job with the official organ of the Citizens Association, one of the first civic organizations devoted to municipal reform and the forerunner of the city's Board of Health. For years reformers had been calling for the state legislature to establish an independent city health department that would be controlled by physicians rather than the corrupt Tammany Hall machine of Boss William Marcy Tweed.

When he was twenty-four and had finished college, Ambrose married Katharine Weeden Jacobs, known as Kate, daughter of George Washington Jacobs, from a prominent family in Hingham, Massachusetts, and Nancy Weeden Jacobs, whose ancestors were settlers in colonial Manhattan descended from Jonathan Weeden. Little is known about Kate or how she and Ambrose met. They eventually lived in a town house at 575 Lexington Avenue, at 51st Street. In the tradition of Kate's family, and a popular custom of the time, their sons were named for famous Americans: John Fremont Ambrose and Thomas Jefferson Ambrose. They also had three daughters, Katharine, Ida Virginia, and Mary.

Ambrose most likely talked and learned about health issues from his two physician cousins, Daniel and J.K. Ambrose. Another physician, Dr. Stephen Smith, who would become a lifelong friend and personal physician to Ambrose, recognized that outbreaks of typhus and cholera were related to the dreadful environmental conditions in the city, where the average life span was forty-one years. City streets at that time were rank with horse manure, dead animals, and all manner of "rubbish" left for scavengers, including herds of pigs, to collect as a sort of early recycling. Waste collection and street cleaning were handled by the Metropolitan Board of Police until the Department of Street Cleaning was created in 1881.

In 1865, Smith, who would live to be ninety-eight, produced a landmark report on the sanitary conditions of the city most likely with help from Ambrose, who, years later when he was an independent contractor, would be asked to develop a plan for cleaning the streets. However, it would take the threat of a new cholera epidemic before the Citizens Association's efforts paid off in 1866 and the Metropolitan Health Board for New York was founded requiring that three of the commissioners be physicians rather than politicians. Smith, who would become known as the father of public health, was the commissioner of the board until 1875. He later founded the American Public Health Association.

Another doctor close to the Ambrose family was George Shrady, a well-loved physician in the city who cared for Ulysses Grant during his final illness in 1885 and who founded a journal called the *Medical Record*, which he edited for nearly forty years. (Two of Ambrose's children would marry into the Shrady family.)

Ambrose later became associated with John Brown, who at the time had the city's street-cleaning contract. Through Brown, Ambrose became educated in how the system worked. Many years later, at the suggestion of the Woman's Health Protective Association, Ambrose drafted a plan for the reorganization of the city's Street Cleaning Department. "His genius for accomplishing whatever he undertook, no matter how difficult, soon became universally known and on several occasions he was urged to accept public office," Shrady wrote. Ambrose's plan subdivided the city into districts of a certain number of blocks and used white uniformed street cleaners with handcarts to remove street refuse. The plan was so practical and complete that it was eventually put into practice by the sanitary commissioner during the administration of reform Mayor William Lafayette Strong from 1895 to 1897. A previous mayor, Hugh J. Grant, had offered Ambrose the street-cleaning commissionership, which he declined because by then he was developing what would be his signature life's work in the harbor.

Helping to Build the City

In the years following the Civil War, New York City was growing rapidly in population and industry. Leaving Philadelphia and Boston behind, it was now the biggest city in America. Capitalism was at its height and the city was booming in banking, trading, and especially in transportation. There was plenty to build to keep up with such rapid growth; for example, uptown past 57th Street was largely undeveloped. While there was much that needed to be organized and built, there seemed a constant war between the corrupt politics of Tammany Hall, the robber barons, and the reformers. There was great wealth and great poverty and Mark Twain gave the era a label, the Gilded Age.

Ambrose, a trained civil engineer, established his own contracting business, J.W. Ambrose and Company, sometimes with a partner, to develop more ways to improve the city. Being a contractor in New York usually meant you needed to curry favors for contracts by paying off politicians, a practice of patronage. It would be difficult to imagine John Ambrose engaging in this kind of kickback, as he spent his life fighting against it. In 1870 when the Tweed ring was exposed, Andrew H. Green, an attorney and civic leader and colleague of Ambrose, was asked to serve as city controller, to sort out the ring's crippling theft and graft. He used his personal credit to cover the city payroll. Green was a civic planner responsible for Central Park, the New York Public Library, the Metropolitan Museum of Art, and saving the Hudson River palisades from destruction.

One of Ambrose's early efforts was construction of the Second Avenue elevated railroad from the Lower East Side to the Harlem River and another section on the West Side between 75th and 189th Streets. At the time these precursors to subways were simply railroad engines and cars operating on tracks constructed over the streets. During those years Ambrose developed Harlem swampland into paved streets and erected ninety miles of gas mains for Knickerbocker Gas Company. For some of these projects, Ambrose had hundreds of workers in his employ and was known as a fair and equitable employer.

In 1880 Western Union telegraph hired Ambrose to install the first eight miles of pneumatic tubes in the United States between their offices in New York. These tubes under city streets propelled mail by compressed air up to thirty-five miles per hour and had been in use in Paris since 1866. Where a wagon might take fifteen minutes to deliver a message between two locations a few blocks apart, a pneumatic tube could do it in two. Wall Street was quite enamored of them. So was the US Postal Service, which would eventually, install twenty-seven miles of tubes, calling the system the Underground Mail Road.

A VISION FOR THE HARBOR

Once established as a contractor, Ambrose directed his attention to the issue that concerned him most, the harbor. By now he had a reputation and friends and business associates who were also concerned with the city's progress as a great port. It was already known that there would one day be a canal through Panama that would create significantly more traffic to the port of New York, allowing access to ships from the Pacific and Far East. The Erie Canal had already opened the port to the west in 1825.

Steam was replacing sail and ships were getting larger as well as more numerous. The crowded port was also badly mismanaged by serving two different cities. Brooklyn was still a separate city, the fourth largest in the country. Since 1868 Andrew Green had been pushing for consolidating the area into one city known as Greater New York. Thirty years later it was finally established in 1898, and Green has since been known as the father of Greater New York.

Manhattan had a monopoly on passenger shipping and Brooklyn dominated in bulk grain cargoes along the East River. By 1865 virtually the entire six-mile Brooklyn waterfront along the East River opposite Manhattan from Greenpoint on the north to Red Hook had been developed. The marshes were filled in, enormous breakwaters constructed, and a continuous line of docks and brick warehouses erected.

However, the shoreline farther into the Narrows, from Red Hook to Bay Ridge, the broad part of the lower harbor leading to the Atlantic Ocean, was largely undeveloped. Ambrose saw opportunity here for piers to accommodate increased shipping with easy access to the Narrows and thus, the ocean, but there was also a need for connecting it with rail lines into the outer reaches of Brooklyn.

A colleague, John H. Starin, a Republican congressman from 1877 to 1881, was the force behind connecting shipping and railroads in the harbor with rail barges. A popular man, he was urged to run for governor, but politely declined. (He and his wife and his son and daughter-in-law were among the few guests at the small wedding of Ambrose's daughter Katharine and George F. Shrady Jr. in 1887 at the Ambrose home.)

STARTING A FERRY TO SOUTH BROOKLYN

Hundreds of steam ferries carried commuters between Brooklyn, Manhattan, New Jersey, and Staten Island. The Brooklyn Bridge, begun in 1869, would ultimately solve some of the problem, once it was connected to trains and horse trolleys. However, Ambrose wanted to get people to the farther reaches of Brooklyn, an area that was ripe for development if people could only get there.

Crowded ferries crossing the East River were the equivalent of today's rush hour subways. Fulton and Union ferry companies were the major lines. By 1854 Union Ferry Company had consolidated a dozen competing lines and made 1,250 crossings a day for a one way fare of two cents. However, it still took a long time to get into south Brooklyn. Ambrose wanted the ferry to connect with rail lines, which, at the time largely controlled the ferry lines.

The New York and South Brooklyn Ferry and Steam Transportation Company was incorporated by Ambrose in 1886 with offices at Ferry House, Pier 2, East River. Ambrose remained president of the 39th Street South Brooklyn Ferry until his death, when his son John Fremont would take over. Plans were to build and lease fast double-decked iron boats. Ambrose's cousin Daniel became one of the directors and afterward, treasurer and executive officer of the ferry line when illness forced him to give up his medical practice. He soon associated himself with his cousin's contracting businesses in Brooklyn, but eventually returned to London partly because of his health and because he wanted to educate his children abroad. He was elected to Parliament in 1892 from South Lough, Ireland. He died in London in 1895.

Ambrose invited the press to see for themselves what his ferry was like. "I will be pleased to meet at our Ferry House at the Battery at 2:30

pm tomorrow, Saturday, any representative of your paper to join us on the short (round) trip referred to (not longer than an hour and a half from 3 o'clock) to whom I will be glad to impart any information, which he thinks might be of interest to the public."

Among Ambrose's supporters in this venture were William Bayard Cutting and his brother Robert Fulton Cutting, grandsons of Robert Fulton's business partner, Robert Cutting, in the early ferry line from Brooklyn to Manhattan. Bayard was also an attorney, financier, real estate developer, railroad operator and philanthropist, as well as an avid gardener, whose home would later become a state park known as the Bayard Cutting Arboretum on Long Island near Islip.) His brother Robert, also a reformer, founded a trade school to teach young men skilled labor. He also chaired the Citizen's Union, founded in 1897 to fight the rampant corruption in the boss system.

To make sure he got people interested in traveling to Brooklyn, Ambrose created a park on landfill near the ferry terminal, at 37th Street and Third Avenue. The space was leased out for entertainment, such as Buffalo Bill's Wild West show, which was set up with many tents and shows for several days. Previously, no space in New York was big enough to handle the crowds these shows attracted. As many as sixteen thousand persons came to Ambrose Park to see the show that featured nearly two hundred Native Americans, cowboys, Cossacks, and US cavalrymen, not to mention Annie Oakley. With two shows a day, the ferry was assured of passengers. (Today the site is occupied by a Costco superstore.)

"WE ARE THE CHEAPEST FERRY IN THE WORLD TODAY"
In 1892 State Assemblyman Charles A. Conrady objected to Ambrose charging five cents rather than the standard two-cent ferry fare, even though Ambrose's ferry route was more than twice as long. When asked, Ambrose said that reducing this fare would put his company out of business.

"Previous to the establishment of the ferry, some five years ago," Ambrose told a reporter from the Brooklyn Daily Eagle in 1892, "the people down there were crying and clamoring for some direct communication with New York. Under this demand we organized the company and put in operation a service that is not excelled anywhere in this country. An enormous outlay was made and everything possible done to equip the service thoroughly. As to our charges, why I—we are the cheapest ferry in the world today. We carry passengers a distance of five miles for five cents and the Union company from here over to Brooklyn (across the East River), a distance of 1,500 feet, charges two cents.

"There are sixteen square miles of territory down there, to which we are the only direct means of communication with New York and the company has been the only thing that has waked up this section and developed it at all. What can be the motive of this bill? There is but one reason apparent to the mind of all alike. They do not want this ferry stopped more than any of the others. One may draw his own conclusions."

That corruption was still rampant in city and state government was obvious, but reformers continued their campaign to change that. When William Lafayette Strong became mayor in 1895–97, he appointed Theodore Roosevelt to lead and clean up the police department.

During these years, there was a constant see-saw from crook to reformer in the city's elected offices. Ambrose was a director of the Merchants Association, founded not just to promote business, but with the goal of improving the city. They had a committee on city conditions, which became a powerful force. Their bulletin was called "Greater New York." While declining public office himself, Ambrose's friends and business colleagues were the movers and shakers of the city not only in business, but reform politics and philanthropy.

Other prominent investors or directors of Ambrose's enterprises included Gustav Schwab, who was on the committee of foreign commerce on New York State Chamber of Commerce and was an agent for the North German Lloyd Steamship Company, a philanthropist, and grandson of a noted Greek scholar in Germany.

Alexander Ector Orr, head of the New York Produce Exchange and president of the Transit Commission, arranged the financing and construction of the city's subway system at the turn of the century. He was a chair of the rapid transit department. David Dows, grain merchant, member of Chamber of Commerce from 1875 to 1890, organized the New York Corn Exchange.

Rufus T. Bush, whose son Irving would later create Bush Terminal, a massive undertaking along the same lines that Ambrose envisioned, for manufacturing and shipping in one place in South Brooklyn, was also a director. (See chapter 9.)

In addition to a passenger ferry system from lower Manhattan to 39th Street, Ambrose established a series of companies, such as the South Brooklyn Railroad and Terminal Company, and got franchises for the right of way from his ferry terminal into Brooklyn and Queens as far as Jamaica. In 1890 Ambrose told a *Brooklyn Eagle* reporter of the plan to connect the South Brooklyn Terminal Railroad and the New York Connecting Railroad. "It is a most practical scheme and one from which Brooklyn people will reap vast benefit. Through freight and passenger service from Brooklyn to all parts of the United States would not only be of great convenience to the manufacturing industries of this city, but would also stimulate growth of the borough. Manufacturers looking for a suitable place to erect factories would be tempted to build them near the line of the proposed roads, as they would have every facility for shipping goods and would not be obliged to pay enormous prices for factory sites."

THE AMBROSE FAMILY CARRIES ON A TRADITION OF PUBLIC SERVICE

By this time the Ambrose children were grown up and following the family tradition of doing good works and improving the life of the city and protecting their father's legacy. The family led modest lives and seemed to avoid the social spotlight. There is no mention of them in society pages of the newspapers of the day, other than the weddings of two of their children, which were small celebrations held in the Ambrose home and the Shrady home. Ambrose's "natural aptitude and education made him a lover of books," Shrady wrote, "and his happiest hours are spent in the quiet of his library, where he had a valuable collection of rare editions of his favorite writers." Ambrose continued to enjoy the Greek classics with his friend and former mentor Howard Crosby until the latter's death in 1891. Ambrose and his wife appreciated the arts, especially music. Two of their children would become singers and for fifteen years their son Thomas, widely known in musical circles, would be director with the Oratorio Society, organized in 1873 by Leopold Damrosch and still in existence today. His sister Mary also sang with the Society as well as St. Paul's Chapel Choir and the St. Cecilia Singing Society at Trinity Church, where she was active in social and welfare work.

Only two of the five children—Katharine and John—would marry, and only John would have children. Katharine, who married George Shrady Jr. (II) in 1887, founded and was president of the Federation of Associations for Cripples, the forerunner to organizations helping people with disabilities. Her husband was a sanitary engineer and served as coroner of New York. He was superintendent of the aqueduct police, which guarded the city's water supply, then located where the main branch of the public library is today.

John Fremont, who married Minnie E.M. Shrady in 1888 founded the East Side Improvement Association, responsible for the development of Park Avenue.

Ida Virginia was a well-known social worker and for fifteen years she represented Fordham Hospital in New York on the visiting committee of state charities, an aid association. She was on the board of the YWCA and Barnard Club. During the Spanish-American War, all the Ambrose daughters served in the Red Cross.

Ambrose's wife Kate had suffered from heart disease for several years and was cared for by the family's longtime friend Dr. Stephen Smith. However, on the morning of the Fourth of July, 1893, Kate succumbed. The official cause was a blockage of the heart valve and edema of the lungs. She died at home surrounded by her family. She was only fifty-five and she and her husband had just celebrated their thirty-third wedding anniversary.

A private funeral was held on July 6 at 4 pm at their 575 Lexington Avenue home. Kate was buried at Green-Wood cemetery in Brooklyn where the rest of her family would eventually join her. Green-Wood was established in 1838 because churchyards no longer had the space for cemeteries. Built on the highest hill in South Brooklyn (now known as Sunset Park because of the spectacular view of sunset over the harbor), it is the resting place for many prominent New Yorkers of the era. It was considered a splendid park, a fashionable place to go for picnics and carriage rides on a Sunday afternoon. (Several of the people in this book are buried there.)

FIGHTING FOR DEEPER CHANNELS

While operating his ferry and connecting rail companies, Ambrose intensified his focus on the port's inadequate channels, especially along the Brooklyn shore and in the Narrows out to the ocean. The port of New York was a great landlocked harbor with 750 miles of docking area, but in the age of steam, ships were getting larger and heavier and they needed a deeper channel to get into the harbor no matter if it was low or high tide. Those approaching from Sandy Hook often had to sit idle while waiting for high tide, which quite often was still not adequate for passage. The long stretch from 28th to 65th Streets "was an undeveloped swampy section, the shoreline a succession of mud flats, with an average depth of eight feet at high tide. This inability to accommodate larger ships was drawing maritime commerce to other ports.

Ambrose felt that to properly impress Congress with the need for a real deep sea channel, no effort should be spared. "With prophetic vision, Ambrose recognized in advance of his fellows the danger of New York being handicapped through inability to supply port accommodations to ships which within a few years would surely be built," Shrady wrote.

Congress was reluctant to give money to New York. The Rivers and Harbors Committee in the House of Representatives complained that New York already got $4.50 of every $5 for river and harbor improvement. Ambrose knew this was untrue and he set out to prove it. He spent a great deal of time investigating their claims and the following year, in February 1898, he completed a fifty-page document he called the "Congressional Appropriations Acts and the New York Harbor." It was an exposition on what the federal government spent for the improvement of rivers and harbors in the entire nation from 1790 to 1896, including tables and a map on which he spent $700 of his own money. Ambrose was able to show that although 66 percent of the nation's foreign imports and 47 percent of exports, or 56 percent of total commerce of the country, passed through the port of New York, and 69 percent of total revenues were furnished by New York, only one dollar out of every hundred dollars expended for river and harbor improvement in the five years ending in 1896 had been allotted to New York.

He also sent a version of the report for the newspapers, which most published. At the time there were more than a dozen newspapers in greater New York. Many newspapers added their own praise and joined in a rare unanimity behind Ambrose. The *New York Herald* restated the argument in nationalistic terms: "The condition of this harbor affects the profits of every capitalist and affects the price of every bushel of wheat raised on the farms of the northwest, of every pound of beef raised on the western plains. It affects the profits of every capitalist and the earnings of every working man in all the land."

Ambrose organized a large delegation of prominent and representative citizens from the Chamber of Commerce, the produce and maritime exchanges, the Board of Marine Underwriters, and the Merchants Association. They set out for Washington on December 22, 1898, and appeared before the River and Harbor Committee advocating for a channel two thousand feet wide and forty feet deep. And thanks to the untiring thirty-year efforts of Andrew Green, Brooklyn as well as Staten Island, the Bronx, and Queens had just become incorporated into one city—Greater New York.

Ambrose made the principal address. It fell on deaf ears. The committee absolutely denied his plea but not for a minute did Ambrose consider relinquishing a project so dear to his heart. He had met with discouragements before and he was a determined man. In the face of crushing defeat with which the citizens' delegation had met, Ambrose went alone to the Senate Committee on Commerce and met with its chairman, William P. Frye of Maine, "and by his masterly presentation of the subject, secured the appropriation that gave New York a suitable approach to its magnificent harbor," Shrady recalled. Frye, a Republican, was a leading force in the US Senate for thirty years from 1881 to 1911.

Ambrose later explained to a news reporter that "the money appropriated by Congress for dredging the outer and inner channels: $4 million for the one and $3 million for the other. Some said that was not enough for the work. Ambrose said it was quite large enough. The amount of material to be taken out of the channels is seventy million cubic yards, enough to fill to the level of the dry land the East River from the Battery to the Harlem River. That is nine miles with an average depth of twenty-two feet. The removal of this material will give one channel seven miles long from the ocean to the entrance of the Narrows, and along the Bay Ridge shore (known as the Bay Ridge Anchorage) the same depth." Speaking from his office on Pier 2 East River, Ambrose said, "The point has been reached when there can be no further increase in the commerce of this port without wider and deeper channels. The tendency for years has been to increase the size and consequently the draft of vessels. It is by so doing that ocean freight charges have been reduced to a quarter and a third of what they were twenty-seven years ago."

A CELEBRATION AT THE WALDORF-ASTORIA

On his return to New York, the great shipping and commercial interests of the city acclaimed Ambrose's splendid success, and organized a public banquet to honor their colleague at the elegant new Waldorf-Astoria Hotel, then located on Fifth Avenue, the future site of the Empire State building. Cutting and Schwab organized the gala ostensibly to honor Senator Frye, but it was obviously for Ambrose. The Produce Exchange, Maritime Association of the Port of New York, steamship interests, Cotton Exchange, Chamber of Commerce, Merchants Association, Manufacturers Association, Board of Marine Underwriters, Coffee Exchange, Metal Exchange, and the Stock Exchange all contributed to organizing and financing the affair.

Theodore Roosevelt, the newly elected governor of New York, moderated the evening's events. Frye was seated on the governor's right with State Senator Thomas Platt on the other side. Others at the guest of honor table were Abner McKinley, the president's brother, United States customs collector George Bidwell, former mayor William Strong, and Andrew Green. Also Charles Stewart Smith, businessman and art benefactor, General Wesley Merritt, Civil War and Spanish-American War veteran and first American governor general of the Philippines. New York Congressman James Sherman (later to become President Taft's vice president), Dr. Henry Van Dyke, Presbyterian minister, author, and educator, New York Congressman Amos J. Cummings a recipient of the

Medal of Honor for Civil War service. One report said that when the dinner had been served the roses were taken from the tables and distributed among the women who occupied the boxes. This was an age where women were not invited to participate in such events, but in this case, they were allowed to be spectators relegated to the sidelines.

President William McKinley sent a telegram apologizing for being unable to attend because of public business but he congratulated Frye for "his devotion to the commercial and industrial interest of the country."

"Since the close of the Civil War," Frye said, "our progress has been the marvel of the world. We have outstripped the nations in agriculture, in mining and manufacturing. Our growth in wealth and population has surpassed our wildest dreams; our home market became the best on earth.

"It ought to be the ambition of our people to make it the best equipped and most accessible harbor in the world," he continued. He accepted the honor of the dinner, but said he didn't think he was entitled to it, and that it belonged to "The persistency and the intelligent advocacy of one of your fellow citizens, Mr. John W. Ambrose, supplemented by the influence of our Senators."

Governor Roosevelt told the gathering that in addition to upright public men, the nation also needs "private men who do their part in seeing that the community's needs find expression in practical form. The next speaker I shall introduce to you is a man of just that kind. With no personal concern in the improvements outside of what is felt by every member of the commercial organization of New York, he worked patiently for nine years to bring about these improvements, and at last sees the beginning of the work which shall make this the finest harbor in the world." Roosevelt introduced Ambrose as "a man whose crowning achievement was that he had procured for the port of New York an entrance channel 2,000 feet wide and 40 feet deep from the Narrows to the ocean!"

Everyone cheered loudly when Ambrose rose to speak, but with characteristic modesty, he played down his own role, explaining how Senator Frye had finally taken hold of the legislature and pushed it through. Newspapers all over the world reported on this event, although details were not always accurate. One report said there were six hundred guests at fifteen tables, others said claimed there were 1,500 guests.

A GREAT LOSS TO THE CITY

Ambrose did not live to see his dream a reality when in 1917 the *Lusitania* became the first ship to enter the Narrows via the new channel. On May 17, three weeks after the banquet, Ambrose died of typhoid malaria. He was sixty-one years old. According to the *New York Times*, "he was sick about ten days, his illness having been caused, it is believed, by the escape of poisonous gases from a neglected ruin near his office on Pier 2 East River." Ironically, the city's sanitation was not yet up to the standards he had helped create.

"In the death of John W. Ambrose this city has lost one of its most public-spirited and useful citizens," wrote the *New York Daily Tribune*. "He had for years been deeply interested in the improvement and deepening of New York's harbor, and it was largely through his enthusiastic zeal and patient work that the people of the city, and finally Congress, were roused to the paramount importance of this question. "All in all," they added, "Mr. Ambrose was a type of citizen which New York is not always credited with possessing. Such disinterested and intelligent service to the public welfare deserves and should receive a word of cordial recognition."

John Ambrose's funeral was held at the Methodist Episcopal Church on Madison Avenue at 60th Street. Because Ambrose was a director of the Merchants Association of New York, the other directors attended the funeral as a body. The prominence of his ten pallbearers affirms the respect Ambrose commanded in the city as well as the nation.

In addition to W. Bayard Cutting, Dr. Stephen Smith, and Andrew Green, they included US senators Stephen B. Elkins of West Virginia and Shelby Moore Cullom of Illinois. Also Colonel George H. Starr, attorney and Civil War veteran captured at Gettysburg who managed to escape from Confederate prisons three times. Also Frank S. Gannon Sr., a railroad pioneer who worked his way up from telegraph operator to run several rail lines in New York, as well as the Long Island Railroad and Staten Island Rapid Transit before being named president of the Montana, Wyoming and Southern Railroad. Ambrose was buried in the Green-Wood Cemetery next to his wife, Kate, who had died six years earlier.

In an effort to express their personal regard for Ambrose, W. Bayard Cutting and Gustav Schwab later presented to his family a life-size bronze bust of Ambrose made by New York sculptor Andrew O'Connor on behalf of the committee.

"The undersigned wish to give expression to the feeling of warm regard and sincere friendship that they entertained for your father, as well as to their appreciation of his splendid services in securing the improvement of the harbor of New York. His memory will not only be cherished by those who had the opportunity and privilege of his intimate acquaintance, but also by all those citizens of this great metropolis who have at heart the advancement and development of their native city."

In April 1900, during the closing days of the state legislature, a tribute of respect was paid to the memory of Ambrose with the unanimous adoption of resolutions commending his efforts. And in its 1901–2 session the United States Congress passed a bill to name the channel for Ambrose.

In 1908 a lightship was christened *Ambrose* and stationed at the entrance to the channel that bears his name. This ship acted as a floating lighthouse to guide ships safely from the Atlantic Ocean into the broad mouth of lower New York Bay between Coney Island and Sandy Hook. Sixty years later, in 1968, after a permanent light station resembling an oil rig had been erected, the US Coast Guard gave the lightship to the South Street Seaport Museum, where it has been restored and is open to visitors. It is a National Historic Landmark.

Protecting a Father's Legacy

In 1913 Katharine Ambrose wrote an irate letter to the *New York Times* because she believed they had slighted her father's efforts in an editorial, "River and Harbor Improvements." She first quoted their line, "This new channel was made necessary by the size of the great Atlantic liners of today, such as the *Lusitania, Mauretania,* and the largest of all, the new *Imperator.*" "From this," Katharine wrote, "one might suppose that it had been decided to dredge the channel after the building of these mammoth ships was accomplished. Such, however, was not the fact. It was in the River and Harbor bill of 1898–99 that the appropriation was made for the new channel. One of the strongest arguments put forth by my father, the late John W. Ambrose, when pleading for the channel before the Congressional Committees, was that the steamship companies would be induced to build vastly larger ships than those then in use, thereby increasing the commerce of our country, and the commercial prestige of the Port of New York. His death followed so soon upon the completion of the great task of securing the appropriations that he never knew how well his judgment would be vindicated by the recent building of the ocean giants above mentioned."

Katharine, who would outlive her siblings and her husband, was also instrumental in leaving a lasting monument to her father in the city. On June 3, 1936, thirty-seven years after the death of John Ambrose, the Department of Parks unveiled a monument to showcase the sculpted bronze head of Ambrose that had been presented to the family by his friends after he died. This was most likely suggested by Katharine as a way to preserve her father's importance to the port. The bronze was set on a plain granite plinth designed by Frederick Roth with a low relief carving of the waves and map of the harbor.

Mayor Fiorello LaGuardia led the presentation, which began with a concert from the Coast Guard Artillery Band and included an address by the commissioner of parks, Robert Moses. Katharine unveiled the bust as "The Star-Spangled Banner" was played. The monument was placed on the wall of Castle Clinton (see chapter 1), which by this time had become home to the New York Aquarium.

Fortunately, Katharine did not live to know that the bust of her father was stolen from the monument years later. She died at the age of eighty-two in 1945 at her home at 328 West 87th Street. In 1955 the monument was relocated to the south wall of the concession building housing a restaurant in lower Battery Park, but in November 1990 the head was stolen. There was no access to the sculpture when the restaurant was closed, so it remains a mystery as to how it was stolen. Sometimes there was a bouquet of flowers in the place for the head.

In the spring of 2015, the New York City Department of Parks completed a replica of the bronze bust that looks remarkably like the original. They had plans to install it at the east side of the Battery, near State

Street, but it was postponed until the Metropolitan Transit Authority completed repairs on the subway station damaged by Hurricane Sandy in 2012. It was expected that the monument would be reinstalled by 2017, once the subway repairs are complete.

In 2003, Daniel Ambrose's descendant Arthur Ambrose, eighty-nine, of Hampstead Garden, a London suburb, said that he had a photo of Mayor LaGuardia unveiling the statue of Ambrose, so Katharine probably sent it to him. When Arthur visited the United States some years earlier, he enjoyed a visit to the South Street Seaport and a tour of the Ambrose Lightship.

Nearly fifty years after the *Lusitania* "christened" Ambrose Channel, the longest suspension bridge in the world was built across the Narrows. It was also the highest bridge in the world so that big ships could continue to enter the port there. Since the Verrazano-Narrows Bridge opened, all ships entering the port are built to height specifications to accommodate passage through the Narrows. Today's enormous container ships have no problem, but the *Queen Mary II* had to be engineered with a rather squat main stack.

Ambrose Channel is a bit deeper today, now fifty feet.

While the bridge was one of the last projects of then parks commissioner and head of the Triborough Bridge and Tunnel Authority Robert Moses, who loved building and joining highways, the construction displaced thousands of people from communities in Bay Ridge and on Staten Island. Unlike the Brooklyn Bridge, designed by a man who understood the pleasure of walking and taking in the view, the Verrazano has no walkway for pedestrians, depriving them of the spectacular views of the city and harbor and the Ambrose Channel. This changes once a year when the bridge becomes the starting point for the New York Marathon.

To this day one of the most stirring views on earth is approaching New York on the deck of a ship sailing through the Narrows under the bridge, past the Statue of Liberty and approaching the lower Manhattan skyline.

8

Lighthouse Kate Walker:
Single Working Mom

A great city's waterfront is rich in romance . . . there are queenly lin-
ers, the grim battlecraft, the countless carriers of commerce that pass in
endless procession. And amid all this and in sight of the city of towers
and the torch of liberty lived this sturdy little woman, proud of her
work and content in it, keeping her lamp alight and her windows
clean, so that New York Harbor might be safe for ships that pass in
the night.

        —KATE WALKER OBITUARY, *NEW YORK EVENING POST,*
        OCTOBER 1931

ROBBINS REEF LIGHT IS ON A HIDDEN RIDGE OF SUBMERGED ROCKS
surrounded by water and fierce currents. It is a mile from Staten Island
on the west side of the main channel into the inner harbor. From 1886 to
1919, the light was operated by a woman less than five feet tall who had
to row her two children to and from school on Staten Island. Katherine
"Kate" Walker rescued as many as fifty people by her own count and at
least one dog. She once rescued a young man and his sweetheart from a
sinking rowboat and then helped arrange a wedding for them on Staten
Island so their reputations would not be ruined by the night out.

Kate never asked for the job, but when she was threatened with losing it, she fought to keep it and became a legend.

Coming to America

Katherine Gortler was born in 1848 in Rumbach, in western Germany near the border with Alsace-Lorraine on the Rhine River, an area that had endured centuries of war and struggle, causing many of its citizens to emigrate. After finishing school Kate married Jacob Kaird and they had a son, Jacob, who was still a baby when his father died. Kate came to America in 1875 with her son, seeking a new life during a time when German emigration to New York was at its peak. Her ship apparently ran into problems getting into New York harbor, and blonde, blue-eyed Kate, now twenty-seven, ended up on the New Jersey coast. She settled in Sandy Hook where she found a job as a cook in the commissary at the Fort Hancock government reservation. There she met Captain John Walker, a Civil War navy veteran and a keeper of the Sandy Hook Lighthouse, who offered to give her free English lessons. Kate knew very little English and accepted John's offer. This led to romance and they married in 1884. Walker adopted Kate's son, Jacob, giving him his own name.

Katherine "Kate" Walker
COURTESY US COAST GUARD

The couple lived at the Sandy Hook Light, the earliest beacon in New York harbor and the oldest lighthouse in the US that is still standing. Sandy Hook is a low-lying spit of land that stretches four miles from the New Jersey coast into the Atlantic, posing a hazard to ships approaching New York harbor. The nine-story lighthouse on the end of that spit of land came with a refurbished frame dwelling with ample accommodations and land on which Kate could grow flowers and vegetables and raise chickens. The Walkers had not been settled in very long before John was offered the job of head keeper at the newly rebuilt Robbins Reef. It would mean more money for them, and Kate could be assistant keeper, for an additional small salary. This would improve the family's finances considerably, especially since a baby was on the way.

ROBBINS REEF: THREE-STORY LIGHTHOUSE WITH 360-DEGREE WATER VIEW

Off the northeastern tip of Staten Island, but considered part of New Jersey, is a small ridge of rocks and mud the Dutch settlers named Robyn's Rift, meaning seal's reef, as the animals were frequently found lounging there. This name was later anglicized to Robbins Reef, and most of the seals have since moved on. It is near the entrance to the three-mile-long Kill Van Kull—Dutch for water channel—that links Upper New York Bay to Newark Bay, today a busy container ship channel. (Here the Dutch name was retained.)

The first lighthouse, erected in 1839 to mark the reef as a navigational hazard, was an octagonal stone tower standing on a stone base and painted white. After four decades of operation, the house was dismantled so it could be replaced by a caisson structure, like an elevator shaft to the bottom of the bay. The house was a new four-story "sparkplug" tower, with the living quarters within the tower rather than separated as in Sandy Hook. The top half was painted white and the bottom portion brown. A small breakwater jutting from the west side of the tower formed a protective cove to help the keepers reach their sanctuary in rough seas.

When Kate and John and their family arrived, the new house had just made the transition from whale oil to kerosene and was considered one of the most modern lights on the East Coast. The light itself comprised nine lamps in fourteen-inch reflectors. Fresnel lenses, named for their French inventor, revolutionized optics by reflecting and refracting light more effectively and making the light visible for many more miles.

The first floor, arrived at by climbing a metal ladder from a boat, included a kitchen and dining area. A shower and toilet were enclosed outside on a narrow ledge under an overhanging part of the roof. The ledge was also used as a porch, or what Kate would eventually call her veranda. Bedrooms, accessed by a winding staircase, were on the second and third floors, with the watch room and light on the fourth—and top—level. This was also the supply room, with kerosene wicks and extra lamp chimneys in case the light needed repairs.

"When I first came to Robbins Reef," Kate told a newspaper reporter years later, "the sight of the water, whichever way I looked, made me lonesome. I refused to unpack my trunks at first, but gradually, a little at a time, I unpacked." John had an annual salary of $600 and Kate was paid $350 as his assistant. Soon daughter Mae was born and the family settled into their new home with its 360-degree water view.

Kate made it into a comfortable home for her family. There was a wooden rocker by the potbelly stove, where she liked to read the newspapers. Some chairs were arranged against the west wall in case any visitors were brave enough to make the trip and call on them. She put pots of flowering plants in each window, kept her woodwork polished and the floors clean, for Mae's dolls and toys usually found a home there. There was also a rope swing for Mae. Kate bought a wind-up phonograph and some RCA Victor records. Her children loved to listen to music and records found from her later years include "La Marseillaise" and "Silver Threads among the Gold," as well as the popular World War I anthem "Over There."

A boat sent by the lighthouse service twice a year delivered coal and oil as well as their pay envelope, but the Walkers had to row ashore for personal supplies. It was said Kate put fresh flowers on the kitchen table every day but this is unlikely, unless she bought flowers on Staten Island when they went in for food and other supplies, or when the children were rowed to or from school. Staten Island was at the time one of the region's largest harvesters of oysters and clams, so there were most likely fishermen, as well as markets for vegetables as well as general grocery stores near the ferry terminal area.

A WIDOW ONCE AGAIN

One winter day in 1890, after four years at Robbins Reef, John developed a heavy cold, which turned into a fever and left him incapacitated. Wrapped in blankets, he was taken away to the Smith Infirmary, a castle-like structure just west of St. George, later named Staten Island Hospital. Kate, unable to leave the duties of the light and go with him, stayed behind with the children and was not with her husband when he died of pneumonia. As John was being taken away, his parting words to her were "Mind the light, Kate." (There are differing accounts of how John got to the infirmary. In one version, Jacob, then in his early teens, rowed him to shore and got help, while another account indicates that Kate left him with the children while she rowed to shore and brought back others to transport John to the infirmary. One of Kate's great-great-granddaughters believes it more likely that she sounded the emergency bell at the top of the light that would summon help from the Lighthouse Depot on shore.)

"Every morning when the sun comes up I stand at the porthole and look towards his grave," Kate later told a news reporter. "Sometimes the hills are brown, sometimes they are green, and sometimes they are white with snow. But always they bring a message from him, something I heard him say more often than anything else. Just three words—Mind the light."

This story has been repeated through time, as a promise to a dying man, but it hides the true heroism of this woman, now forty-two years old, with two children to support and once again alone in the world. It is the stuff of legend to say Kate fulfilled a promise to her dying husband, but at the time she had no idea whether or not she would be able to. The Lighthouse Department ordered her to leave but she refused. As a single woman in a time when women had few choices, Kate wanted and needed to keep that job, even though she may have preferred living in a less isolated place. She made the best of a situation she had not chosen, and it is likely that she lobbied hard to get the job as head keeper.

The job was offered to men, but they all turned it down, claiming it was too lonely an outpost. The lighthouse service may have doubted that a woman four-foot-ten with two dependent children could handle the job, but they should have realized that by this time she had had plenty of experience, and that there were quite a few female lighthouse keepers in the nation—although none were completely surrounded by water as Kate was.

LIGHTHOUSE KEEPING WAS AN EARLY PAYING JOB FOR WOMEN

While many women were in the lighthouse service by the mid-1800s, it was rare to find one at an offshore lighthouse. More commonly women served as unofficial keepers at land-based lights while their husbands, the actual appointed keepers, were engaged in other paid work. Ida Lewis became keeper of Lime Rock in Newport, Rhode Island harbor, after the death of her parents. Lime Rock was only 220 yards off shore and large enough to include a small house and yard next to the light. Because this was the Gilded Age and Newport was the summer home of many of New York's wealthiest citizens, the Lime Rock lighthouse was a landmark among the fancy yachts filling the harbor. Ida also became a celebrity after some well publicized rescues of eighteen men (some prominent) and one sheep. She was eventually visited by nearly everyone who vacationed in Newport, including General William Tecumseh Sherman and former President Ulysses Grant, both of whom were New York residents.

Staten Island was no Newport, although the ferry, which had been operating since 1817, brought visitors. For a time it was a fashionable place for the wealthy to build mansions along the hilly area facing Manhattan. Todt Hill was the highest peak on the shore between Maine and Florida. It attracted yachtsmen and was also home to a popular baseball field. But mostly this was an industrial waterway of freighters, tugs, and fishing boats. There is no record of celebrities visiting Kate, but over the years a few news reporters made the trek to Robbins Reef.

Kate read the newspapers and would have been aware of these women, and certainly of the well-publicized Ida Lewis. She would also have learned about them through the maritime grapevine, as well. The Lighthouse Department had a depot on the Staten Island shore near the ferry terminal where Kate most likely visited when she went ashore for supplies and chatted with the staff. The depot was the storage, supply, and maintenance center for the US Lighthouse Service's Third District, which included New Jersey, New York, and much of the Hudson River.

By the early twentieth century 211 women had been appointed lighthouse keepers and twice that number were assistant keepers, according to *The Keeper of Lime Rock* by Lenore Skomal. Perhaps it was the job title itself—*lighthouse keeper*, largely about *housekeeping*—that relaxed the men-only rules. It required cleaning windows and lenses, polishing the brass, tinkering with wicks and keeping the place tidy, traditional women's work. Also traditional, the women were paid less than the men. In 1867 Congress fixed the average annual salary of a lighthouse keeper at $600. (That year, Ida Lewis, also a slightly built woman, was finally appointed official keeper at the exceptional salary of $750 a year, twice what had been paid to her ailing mother, who had originally taken over for her father.)

Kate worked at Robins Reef on the assistant's wages for four years until finally appointed in 1894 as acting keeper. The following year she was made permanent keeper at an annual salary of $600.

DAILY LIFE OF A HOUSEKEEPER

As Kate explained to a reporter from the *New York Times*, who had been rowed out to visit, aside from minding the light, there was "as much housework to do here as at the Waldorf!" The reporter noted it had "five large rooms quite as commodious as they would expect to find in a forty dollar a month flat."

"It was a tough job," Kate told the reporter. "Each day I row the children to school, weather permitting, record the weather in the logbook, polish the brass and clean the lens."

When the Lighthouse Board was founded in 1852 it distributed written instructions to keepers. "The keeper is responsible for the care and management of the light, and for the station in general. He [*sic*] must enforce careful attention to the duty on the part of his assistants; and the assistants are strictly enjoined to render prompt obedience to his lawful orders. Keeper must visit the light at least twice during the night between 8 pm and sunrise; and on stormy nights, the light be constantly looked after."

The light had to be lit each night right after the gunfire from Governors Island at the other end of the harbor signaled sunset. "This lamp in the tower," she noted, "it is more difficult to care for than a family of children. It need not be wound more than once in five hours, but I wind it every three hours so as to take no chances. The winding was necessary to keep the lens rotating. In addition she had to trim the wicks and refill the oil reservoir. During the winter, ice would often accumulate on the lantern room glass and would need to be constantly scraped, in order that the light signal not diminish.

"In nineteen years that light has never disappointed sailors who have depended upon it," Kate said. "Every night I watch until 12 o'clock. Then, if all is well, I go to bed leaving my assistant in charge." Kate always referred to Jacob as her assistant rather than her son, another sign that she was quite savvy and professional about her job. As Jacob matured, he began to help with the tasks and was later made her paid assistant.

"I am always up to put the light out at sunrise," she said. "Then I post my log from which monthly reports to the Government are made out. We have to put everything down, from the amount of oil consumed to the state of the weather, and every month I polish the lenses. The latter is a two days' job." Rather than one large curved or flat lens, the Fresnel lens was made up of many small lenses.

On foggy nights Kate got no sleep at all. She would go down to the basement and start the engine, which activated a foghorn that sent out signals at three-second intervals, and could be heard for miles. If the machinery broke, Kate or Jacob would climb to the top of the tower and ring a bell by hand until someone from the Lighthouse Depot on shore came out to repair the equipment.

While the government supplied her with coal and kerosene, Kate was on her own for wood. According to the *Times* reporter, she and Jacob could be seen gathering up logs that drifted out from the shore. When a good log came along, they might harpoon it, then lasso it with rope cowboy-style. Kate could then dry out the wood and use it for kindling in her stove.

A Dangerous Part of the Job

Besides keeping the lighthouse in fine order, the job mandated that "It is the duty of light keepers to aid wrecked persons as far as lies in their power," and promptly report any shipwrecks. When Kate saw or heard distressed vessels, she rowed out to assist them and is credited with saving fifty lives, far more than those reported for Ida Lewis. Unlike Newport Harbor, the Kill Van Kull can be treacherous with its swift-moving currents and tides.

Kate went up and down an iron ladder to get to her boat. Given the style of dress at the time, she was doing this with a long dress and shoes with heels. She did have foul weather gear, however, a rubberized canvas coat and hat—the sou'wester—to wear when she went out in the boat. One day, she noticed a wooden crate float by and rushed down the ladder to catch it before it drifted further, for there was a baby in the box. The infant was not alive, but Kate rowed over to Staten Island and brought it to the coroner.

Most rescues were fishermen whose boats were blown onto the reef by sudden storms. "Generally, they joke and laugh about it. I've never made up my mind whether they are courageous or stupid," she told a reporter. "Maybe they don't know how near they have come to their Maker, or perhaps they know and are not afraid. But I think that in the adventure they haven't realized how near their souls have been to taking flight from the body."

A rescue Kate often talked about was a little dog. When a schooner struck the reef, Kate launched her dinghy and took the five crewmen aboard along with a small Scottie dog whose survival pleased her greatly. She caught the dog between her oars as he was drifting by and hauled him into the boat. "He crouched shivering against my ankles. I'll never forget the look in his big brown eyes as he raised them to mine." When she reached the lighthouse, Kate carried the dog inside her coat as she climbed up the wet and slippery ladder to the kitchen and placed him on the floor. The dog immediately fell over as if dead and Kate quickly reached over to the coffee pot she always kept hot in stormy weather, and poured some down the dog's throat. "Then his eyes opened, and there was that same thankful look he had given me in the boat." A week later, the captain returned to retrieve the dog. As he was being carried down the lighthouse ladder, the Scottie looked up and whined. "It was then I realized that dogs really weep, for there were tears in the Scottie's eyes. It is strange that one of the most pleasant memories I have of my more than thirty years in the lighthouse should be the loving gratitude of a dog."

Another often-told rescue story was of a young man who had taken his girlfriend out for a row on a summer afternoon but didn't pay attention to the tides, which can be quite fierce near the Kill Van Kull. The boat was swept away towards Robbins Reef, where Kate was able to pull them to shore. By now it was late at night and the girl was worried about how she would explain being out all night with the young man, not something that was socially acceptable at the time. The young man suggested they get married, in order to save her reputation. At first, the young woman demurred, but then one of Mae's friends happened to row out for a visit and offered to take the couple to shore where they could get married and thus save her reputation.

Kate had experienced a few violent storms and told of a time when she opened the door and was flung backward as the door slammed against her. Another try, but it hurled her back again. The third time she fell and crawled along the stone pier to the side where the boat was hung. "Every moment I felt I would be swept to sea by the waves," she told a reporter. "The wind nearly whirled me off the landing into the sea and I had to fight for breath. The sleet froze on me." Finally Kate managed to tie the boat fast so that it could not move.

A reporter from *Harper's Weekly* magazine later asked Kate if she was afraid of storms. "Oh, no, never. The storms don't amount to much. Once we were worried—about ten years ago when the bay was jammed solid with ice from here to the Jersey shore, and the ice was piled high as the railing of the platform here. We were cut off from the shore for a week and we thought maybe the lighthouse would be swept away, but it came out alright."

In its 130 years, the light has withstood many storms. Fortunately, Kate didn't live to experience Hurricane Sandy in 2012, which nearly destroyed her former home. An enormous wave hit the back door of the house, which consisted of an interior wooden door and an exterior steel storm door, tore both from the hinges and blew them across Kate's first-floor sitting room. Waves tore up her wood floor, flooded the cellar, and destroyed the generator. The storm even dislodged the granite steps to the front door, as well as the railings and part of the caisson itself.

FAMILY AND FRIENDS VISIT (SOMETIMES)

When you are living in the middle of a large body of water, visitors don't often drop in to pay a friendly call. Kate had few callers, and one relative from Brooklyn who came to visit became paralyzed with fright about halfway up the iron ladder on the outside of the lighthouse leading up from the water.

While Kate did not have a yard and garden as she did in Sandy Hook, she created a pleasant space on the narrow rock terrace at the base of the lighthouse. She considered this her veranda and spent a lot of time there regardless of the weather. She also liked to serve tea there to her visitors in summer, when an awning provided shelter from the sun. Kate set up a table and chairs and entertained out there. According to the *New York Times* reporter, Kate's friend from Staten Island, Alderman Kerrigan, described it as "the most comfortable and coolest roof-garden in New York." (This may have been James or William Kerrigan, both Civil War veterans and Staten Island residents, who might have known the Walkers when John was alive.)

After several years, Kate was more at home in the lighthouse than on land, and she was well acquainted with her nearest neighbors, the boats that passed by her kitchen window. Late in her career, she recalled a trip she made to Manhattan where she had to go twice a year on lighthouse business. "I am in fear from the time I leave the ferryboat. The street cars bewilder me and I am afraid of automobiles. Why, a fortune wouldn't tempt me to get into one of those things!"

For most of her thirty-three years at the light, Kate spent Christmas alone. Even in the early years when the children were young, she sent them to be with friends on shore for the holiday, saying they needed to have some fun, while she stayed with the light. Mae was Kate's primary companion for most of her childhood, but she eventually boarded with a family in Staten Island during the week to make it easier for her to go to high school. She returned on weekends and holidays. When Jacob married, he and his wife, Loretta, and their children lived there for a few years until their children began school. They moved to a house on Victory Boulevard near the shore and could see the lighthouse from their kitchen window. Jacob split his time at the lighthouse with other work.

In 1905, Kate told a news reporter, "I have no time to get lonesome. I have meals to get regularly, although there is often nobody but myself here to eat them. Then there are the beds to make, the floors to scrub, the windows to clean."

After thirty-three years at the light and now seventy-one, Kate retired in 1919. Fortunately, there was a pension, for in 1896 President Grover Cleveland made lighthouse keepers civil servants. Kate moved into a small cottage with a garden at 53 Brook Street in Tompkinsville, Staten Island. Jacob took over the keeper's duties until 1921.

Whenever she could Kate would visit the light to call on the new keepers and it is said, just to "listen to the cry of the seabirds and the lapping of the waves on shore."

Kate died in 1931 at eighty-four and is buried in Ocean View cemetery on Staten Island. Her daughter Mae who died at fifty-three was later buried there with her. When Jacob's wife died at a young age, Mae took on the task of raising her nieces and nephews, and never married herself. Kate has several great-great-great-grandchildren on Staten Island.

It Takes Three Men to Replace Kate

When the Coast Guard took over the Lighthouse Department and assumed responsibility for Robbins Reef in 1939, a three-man crew lived in the lighthouse to perform the duties handled by the diminutive Kate Walker. Ultimately it was automated and unoccupied for forty-five years. But Kate's name lives on. In 1996, the Coast Guard launched the *Katherine Walker*, a 175-foot keeper class buoy tender, which also served in the 9/11 boatlift (see chapter 11).

In 2011 the Noble Maritime Collection at Sailor's Snug Harbor in Staten Island took on the task of restoring the lighthouse over the following ten years. The first level will be museum for tourists and school groups and over the next ten years plans are to make the upstairs into a bed and breakfast.

In 2015 Noble opened an exhibition about Robbins Reef and Kate that displayed some of her furnishings along with many photos of a smiling Kate with her family and friends at the lighthouse. Some of her phonograph records are there, and other artifacts saved by her descendants.

Captains and harbor pilots still refer to the lighthouse as Kate's Light.

9

Irving Bush's Folly

*In him there is a happy blending of imagination, great executive abil-
ity, mastery of detail, with a boundless capacity for work. I am one of
his ardent admirers, and as I once said, and still maintain, Irving T.
Bush is a great asset to the United States.*
—Thomas A. Edison, 1928

When Irving T. Bush was a boy, he liked to visit the Brooklyn
waterfront with his father. The two would ride out on a morning in their
horse-drawn buggy, from their home on 202 Columbia Heights, the area
that today is adjacent to the Brooklyn Heights Promenade.

"The back windows looked out on the harbor and its ever-changing
panorama," Bush wrote in his 1928 memoir, *Working with the World*. As
he watched the shipping in New York harbor, Bush recalled, "I think
I used to dream of the Bush Terminal." Before the Brooklyn-Queens
Expressway was built, the backs of these brownstone homes had two-
level gardens facing the harbor, often with a stairway connecting them.
At the time Columbia Heights was known as Millionaire's Row with
residents such as the Pierreponts, Lows, and Squibbs.

After his father's untimely death in 1890, at the age of fifty, from
an accidental overdose of aconite or wolf's bane, a poisonous plant, the
young Bush, then twenty-one, used some of his inheritance to build the
first warehouse on the water's edge, and thus began what would become
the world's first industrial park, providing manufacturing, storage, and

transportation—via rail and water—all in one place, and establishing the importance of South Brooklyn in New York harbor.

FROM AN OLD DUTCH FAMILY

Bush's father Rufus had provided a strong role model. He was a self-made man and a natural salesman who grew up in rural New York State. His family directly descended from Ter Bosch, who emigrated from Amsterdam in 1662. The "T" in the middle of the Bush names is for Ter, and all the family were lifelong members of the Holland Society of New York. Early in life, Rufus Bush had moved with his parents from their farm in Tompkins County, New York, to Ridgeway, Michigan, a small town southwest of Detroit. After graduating from college, he and his wife worked as schoolteachers for two years. Rufus then became a sewing machine salesman and an early proponent of using direct mail to sell wire laundry line. His business prospered before coming to New York with his wife Sarah Melinda Hall, whom he met in Michigan, and their two sons, Wendell, born in 1866, and Irving, in 1869.

Irving T. Bush, 1917
LIBRARY OF CONGRESS

In New York, Rufus invested with a partner in the oil refining business, Bush and Denslow at 25th Street on the south Brooklyn waterfront. Oil refining involved transportation and Rufus Bush became a vocal critic of the Standard Oil Company for exploiting their customers by controlling how oil was transported. He publicly testified against the oil company's practice of rebates that gave them control of the railroads. (The famous muckraking journalist Ida Tarbell later published his testimony verbatim in her 1904 landmark book, *The History of the Standard Oil Company*, but Bush would not live to see it.) Standard Oil tried to buy Bush off so he would not testify, but it didn't work. Eventually they settled with him and bought his waterfront site for a sum that allowed Rufus to retire. His son Irving would later buy it back and it would become part of Bush Terminal.

While Rufus's business savvy and integrity made him rich, it was a yacht race that made him world famous. When he retired he had a luxurious sailing yacht, the *Coronet*, built in Brooklyn and it won a race across the Atlantic to Ireland against the *Dauntless*, then owned by Caldwell Colt, the son of the inventor of the revolver. Bush delayed the race for two days to honor the death of Henry Ward Beecher, the famous preacher of Plymouth Church in Brooklyn Heights, where he and his family were active members. The yachts set off on March 12, 1887, from Owl's Head on the Bay Ridge shore. Although Bush was a member of the New York Yacht Club, he was not a sailor except as a passenger and left the race to the professionals. The entire front page of the *New York Times* was devoted to the results of that race. Another story reported how Bush had decided to sell the yacht for twice what he paid for it the day after the race because it was then most valuable. But before he let it go, he circumnavigated the globe with his family, which introduced his sons to the wider world.

AN EARLY VENTURE WITH EDISON

The Bush sons would go on to have distinguished careers of their own, and Irving would own several yachts. He was educated at the Hill School, known as the family boarding school for young boys and men, in Pottstown, Pennsylvania, outside of Philadelphia. He joined his father's firm when he was nineteen and also worked as a clerk for Standard Oil for a short time, but his vision for what would become Bush Terminal compelled him to action.

The family inheritance from Rufus was $2 million, the twenty-first-century equivalent of about $500 million, which his sons formed into the Bush Company, with Irving as president and Wendell as vice president. One early investment was forming the Continental Commerce Company in order to buy the exclusive rights to show Thomas Edison's kinetoscopes overseas and to open the first kinetoscope parlor in London, to show prizefighting films. These early movies were viewed by one person at a time winding the film while peering into a screen, and preceded the films shown to large audiences in theaters. This apparently made Edison a lifelong admirer of the young Mr. Bush.

By age twenty-one, Irving could have retired. Instead, he had some ideas of his own. Bush was ambitious, energetic, had great foresight, and wasn't afraid to take a chance. In addition to becoming a force in the harbor, the tall and good looking Bush would become a prolific writer, a man always in the news, a world traveler, a patron of the arts, and with three marriages would lead a rather chaotic personal life.

His brother was not interested in the business, for Wendell by now was establishing his career as a philosopher. After completing his MA at Harvard with Henry James, he won a doctorate in 1905 at Columbia College, where he studied with John Dewey. Wendell focused on the sociology of religion and was on his way to a distinguished thirty-plus-year career as a professor of philosophy at Columbia University.

Shortly after his father died, Irving Bush had gone back to Michigan, where they had ties with relatives and friends, to marry Belle Barlow, a music teacher with whom he would have two daughters, Beatrice T., born in 1895 and Eleanor T., born in 1898. By 1906 their fifteen-year marriage was in trouble and they divorced. Belle and their daughters, then ages eight and eleven, moved to southern California. As a result, Bush did not see his daughters often. The following year, he married Maude Howard Beard, the widow of Francis D. Beard, director of the Brooklyn Wharf and Warehouse Company. Maude was the daughter of Joe Howard, a reporter who was notorious for his gold rush hoax story during the Civil

War. They would have a son, Rufus T. Bush II, named for Bush's father, and he would also gain a stepson, Francis D. Beard. The family lived in suburban Lakewood, New Jersey, and also 28 East 64th Street.

Bush's mother, Sarah, in an era when women had few legal rights, apparently did not object to her son's gamble with what might have been their only support. She was a well-loved and respected member of the Brooklyn Heights community. In April 1913, on her way back from a vacation on the West Coast where she had gone to avoid the cold winter and probably to visit her granddaughters, she became ill and was treated in a hospital in Chicago. Irving and Wendell rushed to Chicago and remained with her until she died several days later. Rev. Dr. Newell Dwight Hillis, who succeeded Henry Ward Beecher as pastor of Plymouth Church, gave a speech at the funeral at the Bush home that moved everyone to tears. A song, "Light in the Darkness," by General Horatio King, was sung. Sarah remained widely known through her charity works.

A VISION FOR THE HARBOR

After Irving Bush built that first warehouse building in 1890 on the edge of the harbor in Sunset Park, he began the planning and construction over the next few years of what would become Bush Terminal, the largest multi-tenant industrial property in the US, covering two hundred acres from 27th Street to 50th Street. Bush added to it despite the naysayers who thought he was depriving his mother and brother of their inheritance. Friends told him that the transportation distance to Brooklyn from other parts of the port, especially from New Jersey, would doom his plan for a rail and water terminal to failure. Skeptics thought such a large-scale idea would never succeed and it became known as Bush's Folly. How would he get all the entities to cooperate with each other? To show the skeptics and get the business started, Bush became his own customer. He sent an agent to Michigan, where he still had connections, with instructions to buy one hundred carloads of hay and try to have it sent in its original railcar to Bush's terminal. Eastern railroad companies declined the request but eventually the Baltimore and Ohio Railroad accepted the offer to negotiate directly with the new terminal company. Others soon followed. Using the same idea to get the steamship lines interested, Bush leased some ships and entered the banana business (and made a profit).

Within a decade, what had started as a single warehouse was becoming a transnational shipping hub. Within two decades the complex originally derided as Bush's Folly became a great success. At its peak it was the largest employer in Brooklyn, providing jobs for twenty-five thousand workers.

Not only was Bush Terminal the first and largest integrated cargo and manufacturing site in the world, it was a model for other industrial parks. It had ten factory loft buildings occupying five million square feet for manufacturing and 125 warehouses to store cargo. It had a truck fleet and its own police and fire departments. In addition the complex operated its own fleet of tugs, car floats and float bridges for railroad shipments, and a connecting railroad line and yard that could handle two thousand rail cars. From 700 to 750 steamships from 20 companies used the piers annually.

The Bush Terminal Company offered manufacturers and shippers a total service—one-stop shopping. By renting a spacious modern factory loft in a Bush building, the manufacturer could eliminate all shipping problems. Terminal personnel would receive shipments at the elevator door and transfer them to freight cars waiting at sidings. Bush engines would move the cars onto carfloats (flat boats with tracks, designed to carry freight cars), which would be towed across the harbor by Bush tugs to connections with all major railroads serving the continent. Alternatively the terminal company could place the manufactured goods on steamships bound for all corners of the world, or on a Bush-owned fleet of horse-drawn trucks for local delivery in Brooklyn or via ferry to Manhattan.

The purpose of all this was to apply efficient organizational techniques to eliminate congestion, delay, and expense of doing business in older facilities. Bush, who had been born in Midwest farm country, was especially cognizant of how poorly produce was distributed in the port of New York. It had to be unloaded, stored, and reloaded, moving from wholesale to retail at various terminals, each adding time and delay. Bush devoted an entire chapter in his memoir to "His Honor the Farmer," about his early life in Michigan.

An enormous new double-deck pier, the largest steamship pier in the United States, 1,400 feet long and 270 feet wide, was constructed there. It had 14.5 acres of floor space and a railroad track in the middle of the lower deck. Slips beside the pier were dredged to forty feet, to accommodate oceangoing vessels without difficulty. As a result, South Brooklyn rapidly became one of the most important industrial centers of the city.

The Merchants Association of Greater New York, an organization that promoted business as well as civic improvement, declared south Brooklyn was now a focus of world trade. "The borough of Brooklyn," they pointed out, "exceeds in size the area occupied by either Boston or St. Louis. No other harbor in the world has so much waterfront, and in no other harbor are the channels so deep and so well adapted for ocean-going traffic," they reported in their bulletin of April 1914, an issue devoted entirely to Brooklyn. The Brooklyn waterfront was now the only part of New York harbor adequately equipped with joint terminals, which provide the combined advantages of receiving, storing, shipping and manufacturing facilities.

A MAN OF THE WORLD, NOT OFTEN HOME

Early on Bush admitted that public speaking "always made me nervous," but he apparently overcame it. He was active and well-known in business and civic circles and traveled all over the United States and the world in search of clients. He wrote articles for business journals, newspapers, and he made good copy for others. Bush was frequently sought out by reporters for the *New York Times*, the *Brooklyn Eagle*, and the city's many other newspapers of the time. He wrote a number of articles for magazines such as *Nation's Business, Harper's Weekly*, and *Colliers. Forbes* magazine included him on their "richest" list early on.

From the get-go, Bush was politically active. In 1895, when he was only twenty-six, he chaired a dinner at the Hotel Astor honoring Charles Evans Hughes, New York's thirty-sixth governor and later Supreme Court justice, and read a letter from President Calvin Coolidge. Secretary of State Elihu Root was the speaker.

As a world traveler, Bush was interested in fostering cultural relations with other countries. Early on he set up scholarships to bring students from Europe to study conditions in the United States. However, with all his travel and building his business, Bush was probably not an easy man to live with. Although his marriage to Maude would last twenty-three years, it was apparently a troubled union. In a diary kept by Maude and later found in a rare book store, she complained about the loneliness and discontent she and "Rufie" and Francis suffered with their often missing husband and father.

Nevertheless, Bush apparently tried to be a concerned husband and father. A notice in a 1919 newspaper column reported that Bush was attending a concert at The Greenbrier, the popular society resort in White Sulphur Springs, West Virginia, with his wife, Maude, his daughters, now young women, along with young son Rufus. In a 1928 letter of response to the Hill School, which had asked him to assist with fund-raising for his alma mater, he noted that he was unavailable on a particular date. "I am sorry I cannot go to the Alumni Dinner on the 21st. One of my daughters, who is married and lives in California, and whom I only see about once a year, is in New York all of next week, and I have arranged to take her to the theatre on that evening." (He then proceeded to inform the correspondent why he was actually the worst fund-raiser in the world.)

HEADING THE PORT WAR BOARD

At the outbreak of World War I, Franklin D. Roosevelt, then assistant secretary of the navy, took over the terminal. Bush complied with government demands and also donated his two yachts to the navy to serve as patrol boats. The navy also purchased his steam yacht *Christabel*, which saw action against German U-boats and garnered a Medal of Honor for a sailor during one of those engagements.

Bush was appointed chief of embarkation for the Port of New York, director of the harbor and terminal facilities, and chief executive of the War Board of the Port of New York. He refused any high military rank, but was commended by Secretary of War Newton D. Baker. He was also chairman of the Committee on Harbor and Shipping of the Chamber of Commerce of the State of New York, an organization he would later serve as president.

In a *New York Times* article of July 21, 1917, Bush expressed his concern about the lack of speed in the nation's ships. By now hundreds of merchant ships and passenger liners, including the *Lusitania*, had been sunk by German U-boats.

"The fact that fast vessels are needed is so obvious, once it is presented, that it seems silly it has not been generally recognized before. The United States is a young shipbuilder, but the American people were the first to grasp the full importance of the fact that speed spells safety," he wrote.

"We know the fast passenger liners are going safely, and the slow boats are being sunk. We know England and France are using their fast boats for transports and are not losing them. These facts alone should be proof enough that we need speed. The chart analysis presented by the Chamber of Commerce of the State of New York brings for the first time clearly before us what many have known but have not stopped to digest. The kaiser and his advisers must have had many a good laugh at our program of building slow boats to run a blockade. They will laugh on the other side of their mouths when they discover we have waked up before it is too late."

As a frequent traveler to Europe, Bush had plenty of opinion on what was wrong in Europe and how little they learned from World War I. "Mr. Wilson said we fought the war to make the world safe for democracy. We have apparently made Europe safe for autocracy and at home we are wondering how to make democracy safe for the world." In 1917 he advocated recognizing Russia and in a visit there told Soviet officials they needed foreign capital to develop their resources.

The Great War, however, had stimulated port development in New York. The navy expanded its shipyard in Wallabout Bay off the East River in the Vinegar Hill area, while the army called on Bush to assist with the design and construction of the mammoth ninety-five-acre Military Ocean Terminal on the Bay Ridge shore from 58th to 63rd Streets just south of Bush Terminal. He was asked to assist General George Washington Goethals, who had been chief engineer of the Panama Canal, and principal architect Cass Gilbert, known for his Beaux Arts and Gothic building styles such as his Woolworth Building and the US Customs House, in designing the terminal to provide the same kinds of access to transportation provided by Bush Terminal. A massive four-million-square-foot complex begun in 1918 was built in just seventeen months and was the largest military depot and supply base in the country until World War II. It was also the largest concrete building in the world. Highly innovative for its time, it was constructed of steel-reinforced concrete slabs and included ninety-six centrally located push-button elevators. Bridges linked the two main buildings and there was a skylight enclosed atrium in the larger of the two buildings.

While the army terminal was more utilitarian and much different from Gilbert's other work, it is recognized by modern architects the world over for its powerful aesthetic. Like Bush Terminal it has today been converted to modern industry, such as Jacques Torres Chocolate Factory in 2014, but this massive cream-colored complex, now known as the Brooklyn Army Terminal, is still a very impressive structure on the waterfront, especially at sunset when it takes on a golden glow and its hundreds of perfectly shaped windows reflect the light. It became world-famous in 1958 when Elvis Presley shipped out from there to his army duty in Germany.

CREATING EARLY WORLD TRADE CENTERS

Bush always had a keen eye for art and architecture and two buildings he constructed as early world trade centers are now landmarks. While the Army Terminal was under way, Bush was building his own thirty-two-story neo-Gothic tower at 130-32 West 42nd Street, just east of Times Square. The tallest building in New York at the time, it opened in 1918 and this recently restored building has been a New York City landmark since 1988. This tall, narrow tower influenced subsequent skyscraper design and was widely praised by architectural critics.

The Bush Tower was unique, a museum concept for commercial space, a showroom, and social gathering spot for Bush's Sunset Park tenants. It was, in effect, an early World Trade Center. No one had done that before. Buyers could see the wares of a particular industry in one place, with individual showrooms in one building, one-stop shopping for wholesalers, just as Bush Terminal was a one-stop manufacturing and shipping enterprise.

Forbes magazine called it a vast centralized marketplace under one roof where complete lines of goods could be examined without loss of time. They cited Bush as "a living example of the type of businesspeople whose industrious, diligent, vigilant, foundation-laying could lead to successful business enterprises."

"It is of, by, and for the buyer," reported *Business Digest and Investment Weekly*, in 1919, remarking that it was "also roomier and more healthful for employees."

The Tower was also designed to be welcoming to women members as well. There were "retiring rooms" for both men and women, buffet service and a reading room. It might be premature to call Bush a feminist, but this was the era when women were finally about to win the right to vote, and women worked in Bush Terminal on equal footing with men and were treated equally in the business tower as well. Bush considered himself a progressive, yet when writing about business in his memoir, he always addresses "the businessman" of future generations.

In 1923 Bush built another splendid architectural gem, Bush House in London with the same architects, Helmle and Corbett. Said to be the most expensive building in the world when constructed, it is a Beaux Arts masterpiece with exceptional views of the Thames. Bush dedicated the building to the friendship of the English-speaking peoples. In 1927 Bush claimed, "I imagine there will be no other building in London containing so many business offices." This is where he developed trade with Europe. The British Broadcasting Company (BBC) moved in in 1941 and remained until 2012. This building, too, in 2015 was being restored to its original architectural splendor.

WORKING WITH THE WORLD

In 1928, Bush wrote a business memoir called *Working with the World*, published by Doubleday Doran. He dedicated it "to the young men of America, who have before them the Golden Age of our nation."

"Through the Bush Terminal I have been working with the world for more than 30 years," he wrote, "and that work has brought me in contact with all kinds of men and women and made me think about the problems of other nations as well as our own."

Praising American efficiency, he wrote, "We build a twenty-story building more quickly than an eight-story structure is erected abroad."

"The inventive genius of the American people has been remarkable," he added. A reviewer said, "It will set your imagination going; will make you able to see the 'Golden Age'" Bush believed the country was in.

The book was also endorsed by Thomas A. Edison, who cabled from Orange, New Jersey. "It has been truly said of Irving T. Bush that no man in the world has had a clearer foresight into the possibilities of the economical management of large public enterprises. In him there is a happy blending of imagination, great executive ability, mastery of detail, with a boundless capacity for work. I am one of his ardent admirers, and as I once said, and still maintain, Irving T. Bush is a great asset to the United States."

Bush wasn't above using his clout to espouse products as a way to promote his book. That same year, a 1928 *Life* magazine ad for Fleischmann's yeast featured Bush. "Grade B Health often the real reason men fail to win promotion," says eminent industrialist Irving T. Bush. The yeast was prescribed as a way to perk up sluggish digestion and the company used celebrities in their ads. Grade B health meant you were not physically up to par or lacked energy. "Grade B health takes the edge off a man's working power, weakens his capacity to meet emergencies, and to stand up under strain and fatigue. As an employer, I consider Grade B Health one of the great causes of waste in industry." Grade B health was a label, not the name of a disease; and in 1938 the Federal Trade Commission shut Fleischmann's down for false advertising.

PHILANTHROPY, ART, AND ROMANCE

"We reached the golden age through industry," Bush wrote in a news article. "Now, American art is coming into its own. It is because of the pioneers of the United States worked that we have been able to accumulate wealth and have leisure to devote to art."

Bush became a founding trustee of Grand Central Art Galleries, an artists' cooperative established in 1923 by John Singer Sargent, Edmund Greacen, Walter Leighton Clark, and others. Also on the board with Bush was the galleries' architect, William Adams Delano, Robert DeForest, president of the Metropolitan Museum of Art, Frank Logan, vice president of the Art Institute of Chicago. The galleries were on the third level of Grand Central Terminal, where they remained for seventy-one years until closing in 1994. For several years, Bush also established an art award in his name for upcoming artists.

Wendell Bush, also a world traveler and art aficionado, focused on artifacts of religion that he routinely bought during his travels, such as reproductions of Shinto shrines, Native American sand paintings, and African sculpture. For Wendell, art cultivated a universal human spirit. The Wendell Bush Collection at Columbia University has some of these objects. In 1929 Irving also donated an award-winning stained glass window to the Brooklyn Museum in memory of his parents. Designed by the J.R. Lamb Studios, it was titled "Religion Enthroned." It had been commissioned for the 1900 World Exposition in Paris and won several awards. Bush undoubtedly discussed religion as well as art with his brother, and in 1927 he wrote what we would today call a "think piece" for the *Outlook* publication called "A Business Man's View of Religion." Bush believed in a higher power, and that all the world's religions shared the same belief while they had different ways of practicing that belief. He objected to those who judged others by what he considered old-fashioned sectarian rules. "I have deep religious convictions. Perhaps not just like theirs, but they are strong and deep. If they point accusing fingers at me, I shall say they have tried their way, and ask if it has succeeded. Isn't there a danger that because of insistence on dogma the young people are beginning to doubt everything?"

Bush had also since the end of World War I been involved in sending food to millions of children facing famine in Europe. Major General Henry T. Allen headed the National Committee for the Relief of German Children in 1924 and asked Bush to chair the New York effort.

It was through philanthropy as well as art that Bush found the love of his life at the age of sixty-one. During the Great Depression, Bush volunteered at New York's soup kitchens, where he met Marian Spore, an eccentric artist who was also an expatriate from Michigan, a former dentist, and a philanthropist. She was known alternately as the "Angel of the Bowery" and "Lady Bountiful," and her art was frequently reviewed and usually considered quite strange or unusual. She used many layers or "piles" of paint on canvases of mystical subjects.

Bush's 1930 divorce from Maude in Reno, Nevada, and remarriage one hour later to Marian Spore made the front page of the *New York Times* as well as the Milestones section of *Time* magazine. At his hearing, justifying his divorce, Bush claimed that nothing he did seemed to make Maude happy. Some months after marrying Marian, a notice in the *New York Times* announced that "Lady Bountiful, who had been doing charitable work among the homeless in the Bowery, has discontinued the distribution of free tickets for food and clothing. Marian had spent thousands of dollars doing this, two afternoons a week during the winter months. She said the hungry and needy were now being adequately cared for by relief agencies, adding that an investigation of breadlines was made this month by private police of the Bush Terminal Company, which indicated her work was no longer needed."

They were married for sixteen years until Marian's death in 1946.

A LASTING LEGACY

Irving Bush worked right up until the end of his life and died October 21, 1948, at seventy-nine after a short illness. He is buried at Green-Wood Cemetery in Brooklyn with his parents as well as second and third wives, Maude and Marian. His brother Wendell died in 1941. His son, Rufus, who had led a troubled life, and was accused of bigamy would die just two years later at the age of forty-two in upstate New York after a prolonged illness.

Arthur Garfield Hays, an attorney who co-founded the American Civil Liberties Union chaired the Bush Memorial Committee, which held a ceremony for Bush's memory in 1950. Sculptor William Westcott had been commissioned to create a statue of Bush, which was dedicated by Helen Tunison, the niece of Bush's late wife Marian. It was unveiled at the Bush Terminal administration building in front of three thousand notables and employees. The lead speakers were Edward Cavanagh Jr., then commissioner of marine and aviation, and later to become one of the city's most innovative and progressive fire commissioners; John Bennett Jr., chief justice of the court of special sessions; and John F. Hayes, who would become Brooklyn borough president.

By this time, however, the Sunset Park neighborhood was one of many falling victim to Robert Moses's efforts to ring the city's waterfronts with highways. The Gowanus Expressway, completed in 1941 along Third Avenue, cut the neighborhood off from its waterfront, and led to the decline of a thriving neighborhood, made worse by the migration to the suburbs following World War II. The terminal buildings gradually fell into disuse. The most famous later tenant, the Topps Company, produced Bazooka bubble gum and baseball cards there until 1965, but the complex was becoming a dark area of shabby buildings and facilities in disrepair.

The Harry Helmsley real estate group bought Bush Terminal complex in 1963, but attempts to add container ports to the site in the 1970s, were halted because of toxic wastes dumped at the site. In 2006 Mayor Michael Bloomberg and Governor George Pataki announced a $36 million plan to clean up and redevelop the Bush Terminal piers—the largest single grant New York State ever awarded to clean a brown-field site.

Today, with sixteen of the original buildings restored, Industry City has blossomed on forty acres of Bush Terminal. What was once the largest multi-tenant industrial property in the United States has been reinvented for the information age; the buildings housing cutting-edge businesses of today's entrepreneurs. Bush would certainly appreciate that his facility has once again become the site of innovation for a new era. Exhibitions, conferences, rooftop movie nights are all part of the efforts to make it a community destination. A fourteen-mile Brooklyn Waterfront greenway will eventually connect neighborhoods along the South Brooklyn waterfront from Red Hook to Bay Ridge. Bush Terminal Piers Park, along restored wetlands between 43rd and 51st Streets offers spectacular views of tidal pools and the Bay Ridge Anchorage. There are two soccer and softball fields as well as a nature preserve.

And the Irving T. Bush statue appears well cared for.

Malcom McLean: Thinking *Inside* the Box

Four decades ago, when the Ideal X *sailed with the first shipment of containerized cargo, few could have foreseen the global impact of your innovative idea. Containerization has created international trading relationships that have fueled the world's economy and helped it to keep its peace.*
—President Bill Clinton to Malcom McLean,
April 26, 1996

In 1937, a twenty-four-year-old truck driver from North Carolina hauled a load of cotton bales to a pier in New York harbor where he had to wait almost a whole day before his truck was unloaded and the cargo stowed on a freighter. Other trucks waited too. As he waited and watched, he was struck by the inefficiency of the whole process, the enormous waste of time and money. Why couldn't he just put his truck right on the ship, maybe take the wheels off and put them back at the other end? Twenty years later, that truck driver came back to the port of New York and showed the world how it could be done. Not only did he change the nature of shipping and the world economy, he also changed New York harbor.

Before the container, Marc Levinson writes in his book *The Box: How the Shipping Container Made the World Smaller and the World Economy Bigger*, "It was not routine for shoppers to find Brazilian shoes and Mexican vacuum cleaners in stores in the middle of Kansas. Japanese families did not eat beef from cattle in Wyoming, and French clothing designers did not have their exclusive apparel cut and sewn in Turkey and Vietnam." Yet, when Malcom McLean died in New York at eighty-seven, few people outside of the maritime business knew much about a man who literally changed the world. Today 90 percent of the world's trade moves in containers and the world's ports as well as the jobs associated with them have never been the same.

GROWING UP ON A FARM

Malcom Purcell McLean was born in 1913 in Maxton, a swampy area of southeastern North Carolina that had been populated by Scottish Highlanders in the eighteenth century. One of seven children of a farmer, McLean's first business venture was selling eggs for his mother for a small commission. His was an extended family with many relatives, some prominent, populating the region, and while times were tough growing up during the Great Depression, the family was not without resources. This budding entrepreneur also changed the spelling of his first name—from Malcolm to Malcom—to reflect its Scottish origin.

In 1935 McLean finished high school in nearby Winston-Salem. His family could not afford to send him to college, but his salary from working at a gas station along with help from his family enabled him to buy a used truck, which he later described as a clunker. With his sister Clara and brother Jim, he founded McLean Trucking based in nearby Red Springs. They began by hauling empty tobacco barrels with Malcom as one of the drivers. By 1940 McLean's resourcefulness—being one of the first to use diesel fuel and locating the most efficient driving routes—enabled him to expand to thirty trucks, and ultimately McLean Trucking grew into one of the nation's largest trucking companies.

McLean did not rush to pursue his freight handling idea for ships, which he knew would require enormous financial resources, so he set out to get rich first. He also married Margaret Sikes and began a family that included a son Malcom Jr. and daughters Nancy and Patricia. The marriage would last more than fifty years until Margaret died in 1992. Years later a colleague of McLean's described Margaret as "a rock solid person" who meant a lot to McLean.

Malcom McLean at Port Newark
COURTESY A.P. MOLLER-MAERSK ARCHIVES

In 1955 McLean decided he was rich enough to pursue his dream and sold his trucking company with nearly two thousand trucks, leaving him with a net worth of $25 million, or about $200 million in twenty-first-century dollars. There are varying reports on the exact amount, but he used his share of the company proceeds and set out to do what he had dreamed of twenty years earlier. Forming a corporation called McLean Industries, Inc. of New York, he bought Pan Atlantic Steamship Company and its parent Waterman Steamship Company, which would become SeaLand Service and begin pioneering container shipping. With a multimillion dollar bank loan, McLean bought two World War II tankers, which he reconfigured so that they could carry containers (then called trailer vans) on and under the deck.

"He had a vision of doing something that hadn't been done before. His vision of, and commitment to, containerization was as clear as a bell to him," said R. Kenneth Jones, chairman of Hampshire Management Group. McLean also liked the New Jersey side of the Port of New York, especially Newark, which at the time was underused, and had space for the kind of facility he would need to accommodate his trailer vans. Most of the harbor's piers at the time—there were about 250 of them in the upper harbor on the Brooklyn and Manhattan shores—had been built in the previous century, narrow wooden affairs, where a modern truck would not even be able to make a U-turn. (And while the city made improvements to create better piers and terminals for passenger liners, before they even completed them airlines were becoming the preferred mode of travel and had taken most of that traffic away.)

Newark was also close to the New Jersey Turnpike, which had opened in 1951 and provided access to the port for trucks from all over the country. With the construction of the national interstate highway system after World War II, the preferred method of hauling freight was changing from trains to trucks.

THE DEATH KNELL SOUNDS FOR AN ANCIENT SYSTEM

Since the beginning of time, freight had to be hoisted aboard ship in small lots and then carefully stowed in the ship's hold in a way that would avoid damage during the journey. This system called break bulk was time-consuming and labor-intensive. Between the crew on deck and crew in the ship's hold, forty to fifty people were handling cargo. In the early 1950s the Port of New York and New Jersey handled one-third of the nation's trade in manufactured goods, and provided jobs for more than one hundred thousand people in water transport, trucking, and warehousing, including forty thousand stevedores.

Anyone who remembers the movie *On the Waterfront*, based on actual events on the New York waterfront, understands how the workers were exploited, as well as the resulting graft and corruption, not to mention the wasted time and lost goods. One of McLean's often repeated quotes is: "I don't have much nostalgia for anything that loses money." With containerization, loading cargo with cranes required no more than a dozen or so workers at a time to drive forklifts, so only four thousand workers were needed in the entire port.

The Port Authority eventually understood the advantage and played an active financial role in launching containerization. SeaLand paid for their first cranes, which look like giant steel grasshoppers on the shoreline, but after that the Port Authority began building the terminals with cranes and tracks and then leasing them to shippers.

McLean's first ship, the 524-foot *Ideal X*, led the way in 1956 with its revolutionary load of fifty-eight cargo containers. Much like the first "clunker" of a truck he owned, McLean described the ship as "an old bucket of bolts." That year, most cargo handled by longshoremen cost $5.86 a ton. Using containers, it cost only 16 cents a ton to load a ship. A container was loaded onto the *Ideal X* every seven minutes and the total loading time was eight hours. This meant that ships could be turned around quickly, thereby saving even more money in port fees and other costs.

On April 26, 1956, with one hundred invited dignitaries on hand for lunch, the *Ideal X* cast off from Berth 24 at the foot of Marsh Street in Port Newark and set a course for Houston. McLean flew to Houston to be on hand when the *Ideal X* arrived six days later. (His strategy for buying tankers was so that they could make the return trip with a load of oil if need be.)

A new SeaLand terminal in Port Elizabeth opened in 1962 and operated on a scale that would not have been possible in any other part of the harbor. Almost all of this containerized cargo moved across the SeaLand pier in Port Elizabeth, through the Kill Van Kull off Staten Island and out through the Ambrose channel. The Port of New York and New Jersey handled more domestic general cargo in 1962 than in any year since 1941, but eventually, the lack of ships heading to the upper harbor would change the face of the entire port.

That year McLean expanded his operation to the West Coast via the Panama Canal using the second tanker, the 450-foot *Gateway City*, which could carry 226 containers and began a transportation revolution that transformed the world's economy. However, the revolution didn't happen overnight. He still had to persuade other shippers that containerization was not only much cheaper but also the wave of the future. The steamship executives of the time, most headquartered in lower Manhattan near the Battery, tended to cling to the romance of the sea, referring to ships as "she," an attitude totally foreign to McLean, who believed that the shipping industry's business was moving cargo, not sailing ships. More resistance came from the maritime unions, which understood that the new system would mean loss of jobs.

Malcolm Gladwell, the bestselling author of *Outliers* and other business books, in an interview on inc.com, used McLean as an example of what he terms "disrupters, people who change the world, despite being surrounded by those who tell them their idea just won't work. He knew he was right and persevered until he succeeded."

FROM THE VIETNAM WAR TO A GLOBAL ENTERPRISE

European steamship companies at first ignored containers as appropriate only for domestic shipping. This innovation had no place along the international trade routes, some suggested. When SeaLand gave a reception in Rotterdam to introduce their service to Dutch shippers at the beginning of 1966, company officials were told to take their containers home. They would soon change their minds and today Rotterdam has the largest and one of the most modern container ports in Europe. (Ironically, fifty years later, it was a Dutch filmmaker, Thomas Greh, who would chronicle container shipping in *Fighting the Tide: The Container Story*.)

McLean would find his first European clients in his ancestral homeland, where perhaps they felt a kinship with the way this man thought. SeaLand's transatlantic efforts paid off with Scotch whisky, something traditionally bottled at home and packed into crates. As a result, whisky suffered massive thefts in break bulk shipping. A crate could be opened to get at this enticing cargo and easily concealed inside the coat of a worker leaving the ship or the warehouse. A sealed tank container of stainless steel was a different story altogether. Now, the whisky was sealed until it was unloaded and bottled in the United States, thus ending a common problem in traditional shipping.

However, it was the disastrous Vietnam War that sparked the global embrace of containerization. For the United States military, getting supplies to the troops was a nightmare. It took weeks to unload cargo from military ships docked at crowded Saigon piers and many other ports were too shallow. In addition, graft and theft was endemic in all the ports, according to Brian Cudahy, author of *Box Boats: How Container Ships Changed the World*. Just as container shipping had cut down on theft in United States ports, "it would keep the military's supplies out of enemy hands."

McLean went to Washington to talk with Pentagon officials, who did not exactly jump with enthusiasm at the idea. Nevertheless, he persisted during many trips and meetings until he convinced them. He promised the military that he could turn a ship around within twenty-four hours. After gaining permission to tour Saigon and other ports in Vietnam, McLean saw firsthand just how terrible shipping conditions of the war zone were, not to mention the suffocating heat and humidity. McLean knew containerization would free the piers and allow military equipment and medical supplies to be transported rapidly to the half million US forces there. He worked out a contract with the government to provide container service to four Vietnam ports, and in a matter of weeks Vietnam had the first container terminal outside the United States. SeaLand was shipping 1,200 containers a month to the port of Cam Ranh Bay by the end of the 1960s.

While the military contracts covered the cost of returning the mostly empty containers to the United States, in typical fashion, McLean saw an opportunity for profit. Perhaps Japan, then the world's fastest growing economy, would be interested in filling his empty containers on the way back to the US. Soon, SeaLand was shipping containers loaded with televisions and stereos to the United States. Other shipping companies caught on and containerization grew quickly throughout Asia with the construction of many facilities, including one of the world's largest in Hong Kong.

Now the revolution was global; shipping companies everywhere began to build bigger container ships, larger gantry cranes and more sophisticated containers. This was the beginning of the era of super ships that would change cargo shipping forever. With this developing competition, SeaLand needed an infusion of capital to stay ahead of the game. McLean had worked with Reynolds Tobacco Company in his trucking days, transporting cigarettes, so in 1969 he sold SeaLand to Reynolds for $530 million in cash and stock. Now fifty-six, McLean made $160 million personally and joined the Reynolds board of directors. That year SeaLand purchased five of the world's largest and fastest container ships.

A FAMILY BUSINESS

When a new container ship was christened in 1972 in Wilmington, Delaware, it was temporarily named *SeaLand Pop-Pop* in a nod to McLean's thirteen grandchildren, who called him by that name. (It was later changed to *SeaLand McLean*.)

Family was important to McLean and his siblings as well as his children and their spouses were involved in his enterprises. Geoff Parker, who married McLean's daughter Nancy, told *American Shipper* in 2006 that "McLean wasn't just my father in law, for whom I also worked. He was a great friend. He always had time for family, and then went on to make that time memorable." McLean also had a good sense of humor, "somewhat wry, but always there," said Parker.

McLean's sister Clara and brother Jim were involved with the trucking business and came along with the new ventures. SeaLand was later described by an employee as a company that reflected McLean's vision and Clara's practicality. "Miss Clara," as the staff called her, was executive vice president of SeaLand until she retired in 1969, when Reynolds came on board. She was very influential in the company and also its enforcer, according to colleagues, as reported in *American Shipper* magazine. "When Miss Clara (who lived to be one hundred) said something, you moved right smartly. You didn't ask why or whether she was correct or not, you did it—pronto," one employee recalled.

"Malcom wasn't a big one for running company routines, and she was the complete opposite," said Charles Cushing, who worked as an engineer and later a naval architect at SeaLand before founding his own firm of naval architects, marine engineers, and transportation consultants. "Clara was an orderly, effective administrator. He relied on her to fill that role for him. She was his right-hand man in many respects as well as being his touch with reality."

McLean was away from the office, busy rounding up business. He hated the telephone, preferring to conduct business face to face. He liked, he said, "to look someone in the eye. You could have a frank talk. That was how they did business in Maxton, NC, where he grew up." He also disliked fuss. He was polite to reporters but avoided publicity, according to an article in the *Economist* in 2001.

CREATING NEW VENTURES

McLean also remained close to his rural North Carolina roots. In 1970 when he was fifty-seven, he gave up his day-to-day responsibility to SeaLand and bought Pinehurst, the famed golf resort in central North Carolina, not far from his hometown, for $9 million. McLean loved to golf and enjoyed being on the land to fish and hunt as well. In 1973, he established First Colony Farms on 440,000 acres of swampland in eastern North Carolina. At the time, it may have been the largest agricultural development in the nation's history. Millions were spent draining wetlands to start a massive peat harvesting operation and build a plant to turn the peat into methanol. Nearby McLean planned the world's largest hog farm, where animals were raised to proper weight then shipped to a slaughterhouse on site. Despite criticism from early environmentalists who opposed McLean's methods, it was said to be the cleanest farm anywhere, and it was profitable.

But much as he loved golf, McLean was not one to "retire" in the traditional sense. He needed a challenge. By 1977 he was also frustrated by the bureaucracy of R.J. Reynolds, had sold his stock in the company, and quietly left the board. "I am a builder and they are runners," he explained to a friend. "You cannot put a builder in with a bunch of runners. You just throw them out of kilter."

His restlessness for more global enterprises is probably what led McLean to the first financially unwise move of his life—the purchase of United States Lines in 1977. It was no longer the largest American flagship line—it had been supplanted by SeaLand—and the owner, Walter Kidde and Company, had been trying to sell off its flagship liner, the

SS *United States*, the world's fastest transatlantic liner. (The ship's glory was supplanted by air travel and has spent half a century in various dry docks. However, in 2016, one of the luxury cruise lines expressed interest in restoring it.)

Now McLean acquired thirty ships, a large terminal in New York harbor, and a network of routes, all for a very small investment. He built a fleet of enormous container ships he called "econoships," which would carry cargo around the world and require less fuel. His son Malcom Jr., who had held various positions in the companies, served as president of United States Lines. Greggory B. Mendenhall, an attorney and husband of his daughter Patricia, was vice president. But McLean had overextended himself, and combined with the oil bust of the 1980s, he was forced to declare bankruptcy in 1985, then the largest bankruptcy in United States history, according to *The Box* by Marc Levinson. Although he put the best public face on it, McLean was personally and financially devastated by the outcome with U.S. Lines. He remained a very wealthy man, despite the hundreds of millions he lost, but more difficult for him, was knowing that he had hurt many people who had lost their jobs.

"I had the big head—I was egotistical," he told a colleague.

Nevertheless, he was not out of the game and in 1991 McLean founded Trailer Bridge, based in Jacksonville, a tug-barge company that today continues to carry fifty-three-foot trailers between the United States and Puerto Rico. His son and son-in-law, who had previously worked at U.S. Lines, presided over this operation.

THE 40TH ANNIVERSARY OF THE *IDEAL X*

In 1996, the fortieth anniversary of *Ideal X,* 90 percent of world trade was moving in containers on specially designed ships and McLean was variously described as shipping's "Man of the Century" and the inventor of "the greatest advance in packaging since the paper bag."

In remarks addressed to McLean, President Bill Clinton said: "Four decades ago, when the *Ideal X* sailed with the first shipment of containerized cargo, few could have foreseen the global impact of your innovative idea. Containerization has created international trading relationships that have fueled the world's economy and helped it to keep its peace."

McLean was not comfortable being feted. "The very few times he went to such dinners, you'd likely find him sketching a new idea on the back of a program," his son-in-law Geoff Parker said.

Over the years McLean had received scores of accolades. An editorial in the *Baltimore Sun* ranked him next to Robert Fulton in revolutionizing maritime trade. In 1982 he became a member of *Fortune* magazine's Business Hall of Fame. In 1995 *American Heritage* magazine named him one of the ten outstanding innovators of past forty years. The United Nations in 1999 honored McLean as Man of the Century and the following year the same title was awarded him by the International Maritime Hall of Fame. That year he also received an honorary degree from the United States Merchant Marine Academy.

As Gladwell pointed out, McLean was the ultimate disrupter." He was "the first guy to spend twenty years thinking of ways to make shipping more efficient. So what made him such a success? He was not educated; he knew nothing about shipping; trucking was considered a whole separate field in those days. Like most underdogs, he was completely indifferent to what people said about him, which is the first and foundational fact to understand about these disrupters." (Which explains why the Rotterdam rejection did not faze him.)

"Successful disrupters," Gladwell said, "are people who are capable of an active imagination. They begin reimagining their world by reframing the problem in a way no one had framed it before." Like Apple's Steve Jobs, McLean believed in his vision. What set him apart was not what was in his head or his pocket, it was in his heart," Gladwell said.

A GLOBAL SALUTE

Through the 1990s until his death in 2001, McLean lived in a residential apartment that he owned in the Pierre Hotel on Fifth Avenue and 61st Street in New York, with his second wife, Irena Serafin McLean. Friends called there regularly. "Malcom was very mellow in some ways when I visited him," Cushing said. "He was very much aware of the impact containerization had on the world's economy. That pleased him—but he was so modest about it that he never mentioned it."

Malcom McLean died of pneumonia and complications of a heart condition on May 25, 2001. Mourners from all segments of the shipping industry filled every seat in the Fifth Avenue Presbyterian Church on May 30. In one of the several eulogies, Cushing described McLean as a "dignified, very correctly dressed, polite, and proper person. But who can forget Malcom at the card table?"

On the morning of his funeral container, ships around the world sounded their whistles in his honor. That included Maersk, which had absorbed SeaLand and became the largest container ship fleet in the world.

Norman Mineta, then the United States secretary of transportation, said: "Malcom revolutionized the maritime industry in the twentieth century. His idea for modernizing the loading and unloading of ships, which was previously conducted in much the same way the ancient Phoenicians did three thousand years ago, has resulted in much safer and less expensive transport of goods, faster delivery, and better service. We owe so much to a man of vision, the father of containerization, Malcom P. McLean."

In 2006 McLean's family and a group of shipping industry leaders established The McLean Container Center at the United States Merchant Marine Academy in Kings Point, New York. Their mandate is to collect and preserve records, photographs, and other items documenting the history of containerization. The collection is housed at the Bland Library in the Academy's American Maritime Museum. It is available to historians, researchers, students, and the public.

THE 21ST CENTURY PORT OF NEW YORK

At Malcom McLean's death, it was estimated that 90 percent of the world's trade was moving in containers. Some one hundred million container loads a year sail the world's waters in five thousand ships. Containers have grown in length from twenty to forty feet and today four thousand can fit onto a single modern ship.

Container shipping was a game changer for the Port of New York and New Jersey. In 2014 the port handled 3.3 million cargo containers carrying $200 billion in goods and the entire port infrastructure has been reimagined. Break bulk shipping has all but disappeared. Stevedores have moved on and tugboat companies had to adapt quickly and redesign tugs with more horsepower and thrust to handle the increasingly large container ships.

Today, the freight traffic, approaching from Ambrose Channel, makes a left turn at the northern tip of Staten Island, continues through the Kill Van Kull, past the tugboat companies lining the Staten Island shore, and onto the modern container ports in Elizabeth and Newark.

The upper harbor has been entirely reimagined with many piers finding new use as recreational or commercial spaces, such as the Chelsea Piers on the West Side. Today's passenger piers and terminals accommodate cruise ships, which have not been replaced by airlines, because these ships are meant for recreation rather than travel. There are three modern cruise terminals: one on the Hudson at midtown, another in Red Hook, Brooklyn, and the third in Bayonne, New Jersey, so they seem equitably placed to accommodate the port.

So while the harbor has been reconfigured, it is still the same dynamic port it always was.

As McLean liked to say, "There are no complicated problems. There are simple problems that people complicate."

Admiral Richard Bennis:
Captain of The Port, 9/11

In Dick Bennis, we had the right guy at the right time in the right place.

—ADMIRAL JAMES M. LOY, US COAST GUARD

ON THE MORNING OF SEPTEMBER 11, 2001, US COAST GUARD ADMIRAL Richard Bennis with his wife Gloria was driving south in their jeep to look at potential retirement properties, someplace they might spend some time fishing. They had always had a small fishing boat of some kind, Gloria said, and especially enjoyed fishing for grouper in Florida. The previous day in New York City Bennis had staples removed from the back of his head from the cancer surgery he had endured earlier in the summer. The admiral had been in the Coast Guard for close to thirty years and he and Gloria thought that maybe it was time to slow their lives—but it was still just a maybe.

At Quantico, Virginia, where they had stayed overnight, they got into their car for an early start when Bennis's deputy at Station New York, Captain Patrick Harris, called. In Bennis's absence, Harris had just convened the morning staff meeting at their Fort Wadsworth Coast Guard base on Staten Island. "You've left town again, Admiral. And something always happens when you leave town," Harris said. Last time it was someone pulling a stunt and getting his parachute caught in the Statue of Liberty torch. But this was no stunt.

Rear Admiral Richard E. Bennis
COURTESY US COAST GUARD

"We pulled off the road and I got the portable TV from the trunk," Gloria said. "I saw the plane hit. This was the second plane, but at that moment I thought it was a rerun of the first one." They immediately turned around and headed to New York. As captain of the Port of New York and New Jersey and commander of Coast Guard activities for New York, Bennis was in charge of the largest operational field command in the Coast Guard. "He drove with the lights flashing. Most people let us go by," Gloria recalled. It was more than two hundred miles to the city. As they were crossing the Potomac over the Woodrow Wilson Bridge they saw a huge ball of black smoke rolling out of where the Pentagon should be. They were stopped at a bridge but once Bennis showed his credentials, they were allowed through. "We drove eighty to ninety miles an hour and the police didn't stop us," she said, although she was frightened by the speed for the two-hundred-mile trip. "They assumed we had to get somewhere." The Bennises got a call from their son Timothy at the base near the Verrazano Bridge when armed officers stopped him from going into their house. "They put guns on him until he passed the phone to them so they could hear from the admiral that it was okay. The Bennises were told to drive to Sandy Hook where they would be met with a boat to take them to Station. "It was eerie. I was scared for my family; I wasn't sure where they all were at the time." The Bennises had another son and daughter as well as a grandson.

"For the next thirty days, he never stopped working," Gloria said of her husband.

Station New York: Where He Wanted to Be

Bennis had asked to be stationed in New York. He was particularly interested because of OpSail, the event that would bring more than a hundred tall ships, forty warships and more than seventy thousand small boats into New York harbor in 2000, and would require creating a special plan for security. Little did Bennis know then how useful that plan would be a year later. While he was stationed as captain of the port in Hampton Roads, Virginia, which he called a dream assignment, he explained to Commandant Admiral James Loy, "I heard that New York was going to come open and I decided to put in for it. Throw me into the briar patch. I knew OpSail 2000 was coming and I thought that was the greatest peacetime gathering of ships in history, and it sounded like a pretty good bone to chew on."

Bennis described it to a reporter from the New York *Daily News* as "the waterborne equivalent of directing traffic in Times Square on New Year's Eve." OpSail 2000 kicked off seven days and nights of celebrations of the millennium and America's 224th birthday. As many as four million people crowded seventeen miles of shoreline around New York harbor to take it all in. When it was over Bennis looked forward to a year of writing about what had been learned from OpSail, while anticipating his next assignment from the Coast Guard. (He had been in New York for two years and it was traditional to be reassigned every three to four years.) It was then Bennis learned he had incurable melanoma, the cancer that eventually invaded both his lungs and his brain. Bennis refused to acknowledge the prognosis that he had six months to live, so he underwent eight hours of brain surgery, had a metal plate embedded in his skull and went back to work a day and a half later.

THE EARLY YEARS

Richard Ellis Bennis was born in Syracuse, New York, but he grew up in Wyoming, Rhode Island, a small town near Providence, with his parents Winifred Turner and Mason A. Bennis and his sister Joyce. Gloria Smith met Richard Bennis in sixth grade. They had a rather long bus ride to school, so became friends. "He made me laugh," Gloria said, but it wasn't until they went to the high school prom together that she realized they were much more than friends. That summer Bennis went on an extended trip to Canada with his dad, who soon realized something other than the trip was on his son's mind. The couple married in 1968 while both were in their second year of college and began a family. After earning a bachelor's degree in natural resource development from the University of Rhode Island, Bennis enrolled in officer training school with the Coast Guard, receiving his commission in 1972.

Like most military organizations, life in the Coast Guard meant moving a lot, which could be hard on families. The Bennises lived in Texas, Florida, Virginia, Charleston, and New York. "Our oldest son didn't like moving; most tours were three to four years, but in Washington, DC, we held out for five years so he could graduate high school. However, Gloria said that by that time they had made close friends, "and it was even harder to move."

In his off-duty hours Bennis enjoyed reading military history and Tom Clancy novels. And he loved to restore cars, especially the original Volkswagen Beetles. As Bennis himself described it to the Coast Guard's historian, "I had a '71 Super Beetle convertible; candy apple red, and I believe in driving them after you fix them. I had my surgery and it was one of my first or second days back at work for the very first time and I almost got run over by a fire truck. I pulled over to the side of the road, got my cell phone and called my wife, and I said, wouldn't it just piss you off if I went through all this, I lived, and I get killed by a fire truck the next day. I mean it's the way it is, you know, you never know."

AN ENVIRONMENTAL EXPERT ON OIL SPILLS

During his career Bennis earned a master's degree in energy and environmental studies from Harvard and developed an expertise in handling spills of oil and other hazardous materials that was well known, especially in East Coast ports. He served as captain of the three largest East Coast container ports: Charleston, South Carolina, Hampton Roads, Virginia, and New York.

In 1992 Bennis was credited with saving the crew of the container ship *Santa Clara*, and the adjoining port area of Charleston by averting the explosion of highly unstable materials spilled onto the deck during a storm, and which could explode if exposed to water. In addition to saving the ship and protecting the crew and surrounding community, Bennis devised a method of eliminating this type of threat and his action led to national improvements in shipping container safety and inspection. He led the Coast Guard Office of Response as it updated the way it dealt with everything from oil spills to fires, explosions, natural disasters, and search and rescue missions.

The Coast Guard awarded many medals and commendations to Bennis for Meritorious Service and Achievement. In 2008 a channel (called a reach) leading to a harbor in Charleston was renamed Bennis Reach by the South Carolina legislature on a recommendation from the National Oceanic and Atmospheric Administration (NOAA). This was the first time a reach was named for a person.

A BOATLIFT COMPARED TO DUNKIRK

But on that fateful morning of September 11, thoughts of retirement and fishing with Gloria were put on hold indefinitely as their lives changed forever. While Bennis directed operations from his cell phone not only for the evacuation of crowds flocking to the waterfront from the World Trade Center, but to close the port and stop any inbound commercial ships and boats at Ambrose Light (see chapter 7). There were already a dozen commercial ships with fuel waiting to enter the nation's largest oil port, where the fuel was then distributed to locations all over the Atlantic Coast. The Port of New York and New Jersey is the economic nerve center of the East Coast with its oil and chemical storage tanks, tunnels, power grids, and container port facilities. It was important to get those supplies delivered, but nothing could enter the harbor until it had been thoroughly searched by the Coast Guard to secure it from maritime threats.

The biggest concern during the first 24 hours was the possibility of more attacks. They worried about the Statue of Liberty, the Indian Point Nuclear power plant, as well as all those chemical tanks lining the New Jersey side of the harbor. Everything Bennis had strategized for the previous year's Op Sail event was put into action, including the possible evacuation of Manhattan and where to set up triage sites.

One of Bennis's officers in a patrol boat described a literal monsoon of dust rolling from the Twin Towers toward the Battery, which became so dark people could not see. Paper and debris were flying everywhere, and what appeared to be the entire population of lower Manhattan was racing inside this dust cloud to the waterfront, desperate to flee the island. Crowds were knocking each other over in their panic to get away. One witness described a hot dog stand in Battery Park lying on its side, and even an overturned baby carriage.

Amid the smoke and dust the Coast Guard used radar to navigate their way around them. Officers passed out gas masks, and unloaded water for people scorched by smoke. They directed them to medical centers that had been set up, and tried to maintain some sort of order with the commercial tugs and other boats coming in to take people off. Terrified people were jumping onto the decks of any boat they found close by.

At the time the Coast Guard did not keep a large fleet of boats in the harbor. They had a few tugs, two patrol boats, lifeboats, inflatables, and utility boats, complemented by the 175-foot-deep class coastal buoy tender *Katherine Walker* (see chapter 8). But there were plenty of other boats in the harbor that could come to the rescue of the thousands of panicked people trying to find some way out of the chaos to get home to their families. Ferries, tourist boats, fireboats, yachts, dinner cruises, tugs, and other work boats were all put into action. Bennis directed his crew as they organized a flotilla of more than one hundred boats, many crewed by volunteers, who brought the people to safety and often brought back much needed supplies on the return trips. By the end of the day five hundred thousand people had been evacuated from lower Manhattan.

The retired 1931 fireboat *John J. Harvey*, which had greater pumping capacity than any active duty New York City fireboat at the time, pumped river water to fire trucks, which could not get water from the broken water mains at Ground Zero. The *Harvey*, which had been retired in 1994, was on the National Historic Register and was maintained by a crew of volunteers. Dinner boats provided floating cafeterias and resting areas for exhausted workers.

Later, this waterborne rescue of half a million people from Manhattan would be compared with the evacuation of Dunkirk in 1940, where allied troops trapped by the German army at this north coast seaport of France had no means of escape other than the English Channel. Private boats sped across the Channel from Britain to the rescue, but that evacuation took nine days.

In 2011 a twelve-minute film about the 9/11 event, *Boatlift: An Untold Tale of 9/11 Resilience*, narrated by Tom Hanks, was funded by Center for National Policy and was produced and directed by Eddie Rosenstein Eye Pop Productions. It is available on the Internet (www .road2resilience.com).

THE RIGHT GUY IN THE RIGHT PLACE AT THE RIGHT TIME

Coast Guard headquarters in Washington was nervous about what was happening and Bennis needed to reassure them. "I would take my little bitty cell phone, and I'd take it outside the command suite and I'd lean against the bicycle rack near the galley, because that was where I had the best reception." He programmed his phone so he had a button for his commanders in Washington and Boston.

"And I'd call them on this tiny cell phone and give them the status report, telling them what we were doing, and that I would call them in forty minutes, an hour, and hour and a half. And I said to the commandant, "You need to know that everything we need to be doing, we are doing. We're doing it well. But we need more people, and more logistics support." The only thing they couldn't really do was demonstrate it to those officers outside of New York because of the lack of communications. Even two months later, as the site continued to burn, Bennis kept up his daily briefing. Finally phone lines on Staten Island were rerouted through Denver. When he got his new phone and called his wife, she told him that the caller ID read Tony's Pizza. "Don't ask why," Bennis told her. "It works."

Bennis told his superiors he knew what he wanted to do and from working with the city the best way to accomplish it. "But what I wanted to know was, was I in fact a free agent? And I was. And at the start I need to know if I was going to have that freedom or were they going to micromanage me. They didn't send in a team to oversee the operation. Instead they sent exactly what I needed, the people I needed. It worked out very well." Bennis himself was never a micromanager. He felt his staff was well trained and if they could not reach him for approval and believed they were right and needed to act then they should go ahead. Pat Harris described his technique: "He would say, 'go make magic and be brilliant.'"

The plans previously made for OpSail included all kinds of contingencies for that event, including an appearance by the president, which occurred a few days after 9/11. When 9/11 occurred, they went through all of those plans. "That's why Bennis thought his cancer was meant to be," Harris said. "Everything we ever learned, we used that day and in the six weeks after it."

Bennis visited Ground Zero often during those days, when the commandant from Washington was there and he accompanied New York officials as well. "The first Sunday afterwards, my wife and I went there with several of our chaplains," he said, "just to be with the folks that were there and the folks that were responding there." His son Tim, who worked for Moran Towing at the time, was helping decontaminate the site, as barges towed away the ashes and other debris.

CHARTING A NEW COURSE FOR THE COAST GUARD

Bennis led a round-the-clock effort designed to increase the Coast Guard presence in the port of New York and New Jersey by 500 percent, changing their primary mission from protection to prevention. He charted a new direction for the entire Coast Guard as it entered a new phase in history.

Until 1996, the Coast Guard had been stationed on Governors Island and some felt that leaving this base close to the tip of Manhattan had compromised its ability to quickly respond to any emergency. Others noted that it would have made it difficult for them because their own families would have had to be evacuated from the cloud of dust. Fort Wadsworth was the right place to stage the evacuation. A Coast Guard utility boat can cross from Staten Island to the Battery in about fifteen minutes.

One of the first things Bennis did when he got to Manhattan and evaluated the scope of the devastation that first day was to put out a call to the rest of the nation's Coast Guard to send everything to New York. He wanted fast boats to be taken out of mothballs and sent to New York to increase Coast Guard presence, to reassure the population they were being protected. They had thirty-eight-foot deployable pursuit boats (DPBs), the guard's "go fast" boats for chasing drug-running boats. These had been mothballed in recent years in Virginia, but have found their element in the harbor.

"Without knowing it, that is what those boats were designed to do, where they were meant to be." Bennis believed they were a very good tool for a public that respects and appreciates the Coast Guard while at the same time believing that "the Coast Guard can't catch a Boston whaler." They got the DPBs early on and "I would have them run from the George Washington Bridge to the Verrazano Narrows Bridge at speed several times a day, just so people could go, 'What the hell was that?' It's the Coast Guard. Just knowing we had that capability gave a lot of people pause, be they tourists or people intent on violating a security zone."

Until then the public was used to seeing one or two Coast Guard white boats with the orange stripes working in tandem with the New York Police Department's blue boats with white stripes. Now they were seeing forty-five or fifty Coast Guard boats. Bennis also made sure that the media carried as many pictures as possible of the gray-hulled, black-striped port security boats (PSUs), so they knew this was a different operation. In the past, such boats were not used domestically, but now they were, so the public knew there was a heightened level of security from the Coast Guard.

In strengthening its harbor presence during the weeks after 9/11, Bennis led the Coast Guard in changing its mission from response to prevention. Security enforcement patrols were brought back to New York harbor for the first time since World War II. Maritime security before 9/11 was a relatively small priority in the overall scheme of the nation's commercial shipping and port operations. Two major exceptions were the world wars. During World War I, with the Espionage Act of 1917, the Coast Guard first designated officers as captains of the port. These were senior officers whose job was to oversee loading of cargo, looking for any possible sabotage at a time when German U-boats were sinking merchant and passenger ships.

For most of its three-hundred-year history, the Coast Guard was under the auspices of the Treasury Department. That changed after 9/11 and, along with the National Guard, Customs, the Secret Service, Emergency Management, and other local and federal agencies, responsible for the nation's security, the Coast Guard came under the umbrella of the newly created Department of Homeland Security. In November 2002 President George Bush signed the Maritime Transportation Security Act of 2002.

By now promoted to rear admiral, Bennis officially retired from the Coast Guard in March 2002, six months after 9/11, but that didn't mean he was finally going fishing with Gloria. He accepted Secretary of Transportation Norman Minetta's invitation to become associate undersecretary for maritime and land security in the new Transportation Security Administration. Bennis's challenge now was to develop strategies to protect the maritime, rail, highway, mass transit, pipelines, and waterways of the National Transportation System at a cost the industry and the traveling public could afford. Minetta, who had called Bennis's work on 9/11 remarkable, said "He brings many hard-won skills into a demanding new environment."

When he took the TSA job in Virginia, Bennis brought along several officers on his staff, including Pat Harris. He worked there for a year before the cancer finally caught up with him. Harris and his family said they were shocked when Bennis died, because he didn't appear sick. On Sunday, August 3, 2003, almost two years after 9/11, Bennis died at Mary Washington Hospital in Fredericksburg, Virginia. He was fifty-three and was buried with full honors in Arlington National Cemetery. There was a memorial service in New York at the Coast Guard base.

"He didn't want people to know how bad his condition was," Gloria said. "He wanted to live. He told me that 'If you stop living, it takes you.'"

And indeed Bennis had long passed the original six months of life that had been predicted for him. He never wondered why he had brain cancer; after the terrorist attacks on 9/11, he told a friend he knew exactly why he had gotten ill. His failing health had kept him in New York at the moment his nation needed him most.

A CONTINUING PRESENCE

The US Coast Guard established the Rear Admiral Richard E. Bennis Award to honor exceptional commitment to the security of the US and the marine transportation system. Among the first recipients of the award was the Port Authority of NY and NJ's security program in 2014.

When New York Waterways named a new ferryboat for Bennis in 2003, his family came to New York to christen it. "We all went," Gloria said, and as is customary, she broke a bottle of champagne over the hull. In January 2009, the *Admiral Richard Bennis* was one of the ferries that helped rescue passengers from a US Airways jet that splash-landed in the Hudson, after a collision with a flock of birds knocked out both engines. Everyone survived, so you could say Admiral Bennis is still looking out for us in the Port of New York and New Jersey.

Ten years after the death of Admiral Bennis, Gloria Bennis lost her son Keith to the same cancer that had taken her husband. Today her son Tim and daughter Wendy and her grandchildren all live near each other outside of Charleston, not far from the Bennis Reach.

Author's Note: Some of the dialogue with Admiral Bennis comes from the narrative taken by the Coast Guard historian after 9/11 with the people involved, which is available for use without restriction.

Acknowledgments

I ALWAYS ENJOY WORKING WITH THE RESEARCH LIBRARIANS WHO SEEM to like a mystery as much as I do, especially when trying to locate information from earlier centuries when record keeping had not been defined very well. There are often contradictions, untruths, and biased reports in newspaper archives.

Kayla Correll and Pat Schaefer at the New London County Historical Society were extremely helpful with the chapter on John Newton. Lou Jefferies, the librarian at the Hill School in Pottstown, Pennsylvania, helped put some pieces together in the early years of Irving T. Bush. Librarians at Princeton University and New York University helped me track down the early education of John Wolfe Ambrose, even though the records were not complete. Jonathan Kuhn, director of art and antiquities of the New York Parks Department, provided valuable information about the re-creation of the monument to John Wolfe Ambrose that will be restored in the Battery.

Thanks also to staff at the New York Public Library, the Coast Guard historian's office, the Alexander Library at Rutgers University, and the Lily Library at Indiana University.

Thanks to Barbara Pezzengrilli, great-great-granddaughter of Lighthouse Kate Walker, for talking with me about her take on how Kate's ill husband was transported to the hospital. Thanks to Nick Dowen of the Noble Maritime organization for walking me through the exhibition about Robins Reef and Kate Walker.

As always, much appreciation and love to my daughter Karen, who made sure I got to a hard-to-reach "on-site" location for research. And to my granddaughter Hilary for digging up some papers from the library at the University of Pennsylvania.

Thanks to Dynamite Johnny O'Brien's great-great-granddaughter, Kristin Agar, for keeping me posted on her discoveries of new cousins; to Steve Barranco for sharing his files on his uncle Victor Hugo Barranco. And to musician and filmmaker Charlie O'Brien, who also discovered a keen interest in the activities of this harbor hero.

My deepest gratitude goes to Gloria Bennis for talking with me about her late husband and the events of that fateful day and its aftermath.

And to my friend and fellow writer Francis "Frank" Duffy, who loved to be viewing the harbor from a helicopter and who shared many stories with me.

I can't begin to express my gratitude to Brian McAllister and Ned Moran, who know the harbor well and spent many hours sharing their unique expertise with me.

Sources

CHAPTER 1: JONATHAN WILLIAMS, PROTECTOR OF THE PORT

Books and Articles
1776, David McCullough, Simon & Schuster, 2005
The Martin Portraits of Franklin, Albert P. Brubaker, MD, Macmillan and Company, 1904
"From Here You Could Shoot in Every Direction," Helene Stapinski, *The New York Times*, August 3, 2012
"How Williamsburg Got Its Groove," *The New York Times*, June 19, 2005

Libraries and Archives
Lilly Library, Manuscripts Department, Indiana University, Bloomington, Indiana, Jonathan Williams Collection including letter from Col. Jonathan Williams on the subject of Fortifying and Protecting the harbor of New York; printed for the Corporation, H.C. Southwick, Printer, 1807, and other correspondence including letters from Marianne Williams
"Armed Forces and Society: The Founding of West Point," Theodore Joseph Crackel, University of Pennsylvania library
Biddle Family Papers, Historical Society of Pennsylvania
Williamsburg Neighborhood Guide, Brooklyn Historical Society, 2000
"Guarding America's Front Door: Harbor Forts in the Defense of New York City," Russell S. Gilmore, Fort Hamilton Historical Society, 1983
Philadelphia Museum of Art

Websites
www.nps.gov, National Park Service publications
http://founders.archives.gov, Founders Online
www.amphilsoc.org/library, American Philosophical Society online

www.SilasDeaneOnline.org
http://famousamericans.net/jonathanwilliams
www.goordinance.army.mil/history/chiefs/bomford
www.usma.edu, US Military Academy website; Dorothy Zuersher dissertation on Benjamin Franklin and Jonathan Williams at US Military Academy
www.rootsweb.com, "Uncle Sam's Prisoners in Castle Williams," *Brooklyn Standard Union*, June 9, 1907

CHAPTER 2: THE IRISH NAVY PART I: THE MORAN FAMILY

Books and Articles
Tugboat: The Moran Story, Eugene Moran, Charles Scribner's Sons, 1956
Tugboats of New York, George Matteson, New York University Press, 2007
Towline, publication of Moran Corporation, Winter 1993/4, and others
"The Tugboat and Its Relation to Commercial Shipping," Eugene Moran, *The Marine News*, March 1931
"The Elegant Tugman," two-part profile of Eugene Moran, Robert Lewis Taylor, November 3 and 10, 1945, *The New Yorker*
"Big 'M' on Wheels," C.B. Palmer, *The New York Times Magazine*, May 17, 1953
"Tug O' the Heart," Marian Betancourt, *Irish America* magazine, February/March 2003
"Moran Clan Reunites for a Day in Brooklyn," Marian Betancourt, *Irish America* magazine, January 2010

Libraries and Archives
The New York Times archives
Brooklyn Eagle archives
"The Erie Canal as I Have Known It," Eugene F. Moran Sr., 1959, The Canal Society of New York State
"The Moran Story: Rear Admiral Edmond J. Moran, USNR (Ret)," 1965, The Newcomen Society in North America

Websites
www.moran.org

Author Interviews
Edmond Moran Jr. and other members of the family

CHAPTER 3: THE IRISH NAVY PART II: THE McALLISTER FAMILY

Books and Articles
McAllister Towing: 150 Years of a Family Business, Stephanie Hollyman, Carpe Diem Books, 2015

Tugboats of New York, George Matteson, New York University Press, 2007
"At the Helm," McAllister Towing newsletter, various issues
Sea History Magazine, National Maritime Historic Society, various issues
"Family Affair," Kathy Bergren Smith, *Workboat Magazine*, September 2005
"Tug O' the Heart," Marian Betancourt, *Irish America* magazine, June/July 2009
"McAllister Looks to Fifth Generation," *Marine News* magazine, October 12, 1998

Libraries and Archives
New York University library, Ireland House oral history collection, Captain Brian A. McAllister

Websites
www.mcallistertowing.com
www.MarineLink.com, "The McAllister Towing Legacy," Patricia Keelem, November 2015
www.ProfessionalMariner.com, "Fifth-generation McAllister Becomes Top Leader in Family Business," Brian Gauvin, August 2013

Author Interviews
Brian McAllister and other members of his family

CHAPTER 4: DYNAMITE JOHNNY O'BRIEN: A CAPTAIN UNAFRAID

Books and Articles
A Captain Unafraid, Horace Smith, Harper & Brothers, 1912
A Captain Unafraid, Horace Smith, serialized, *New York Tribune*, February 1912
Tugboat: The Moran Story, Eugene Moran, Charles Scribner's Sons, 1956, Chapter 18: "Waterfront Personalities"
A Ship to Remember: The Maine and the Spanish-American War, Michael Blow, William Morrow and Company, 1992
The Battleship Maine: A Key West Legacy, Joseph Pais, Key West Art and Historical Society, 1996
The Jose Marti Reader: Writings on the Americas, Ocean Press, 1999
"Dynamite Johnny O'Brien," Marian Betancourt, *Irish America* magazine, December/ January 2003

Libraries and Archives
The Chancellor Robert R. Livingston Masonic Library, New York, NY
State of New Jersey Department of Health and Senior Services, vital statistics
Department of Health, New York City vital records
City Island Nautical Museum, New York
County Historian, Monroe County Library, Key West, Florida

Author Interviews

Stephen Barranco, descendant of the late Victor Hugo Barranco, representative of the Cuban Government and friend of Johnny O'Brien

Kristin Agar, great-granddaughter of Johnny O'Brien

The late Ed Mueller, maritime historian, Jacksonville, Florida

CHAPTER 5: JOHN NEWTON, THE MAN WHO OPENED HELL'S GATE

Books and Articles

"The Improvement of East River and Hell Gate," General John Newton, Chief of Engineers, US Army, *Popular Science Monthly*, Volume 28, February, 1886

"Sketch of General John Newton," *Popular Science Monthly*, Volume 29, October 1886

"Hellgate's Infamous Past," two-part series by Claude Rust, *The Military Engineer*, 1971

The Great Bridge, David McCullough, Simon and Schuster, 1972

"The Hell Gate," Chapter 7, *At Sea in the City: New York from the Water's Edge*, William Kornblum, Algonquin Books, 2013

Libraries and Archives

Brooklyn Eagle archives

The New York Times archives

New London County Historical Society

Fifth Annual Report of the State Cabinet of Natural History of New York, 1852

"Memoir of John Newton (1823-1895)," Cyrus B. Comstock, read before the National Academy, November 13, 1901, National Academy archives

Websites

www.encyclopediavirginia.org

www.nan.usace.army.mil, "The Conquest of Hell Gate," US Army Corps of Engineers

www.newyorkhistory.info/Hell-Gate/

CHAPTER 6: EMILY WARREN ROEBLING AND THE GREAT BRIDGE

Books and Articles

The Great Bridge, David McCullough, Simon and Schuster, 1972

Silent Builder: Emily Warren Roebling and the Brooklyn Bridge, Marilyn Weigold, Associated Faculty Press, 1984

"How Emily Warren Roebling Helped Save and Complete the Brooklyn Bridge," *New York Daily News*, May 24, 2012

Libraries and Archives

Brooklyn Eagle archives

The New York Times archives

"The Confluence of Allegory and Technology in Gendered Public Space: Emily Roebling and the construction of the Brooklyn Bridge," by John A. Stuart, Florida International University, 84th Annual Meeting, 1996, Association of Collegiate Schools of Architecture
The Alexander Library, Rutgers University, New Brunswick, New Jersey: letters between Emily Roebling and her son John, Washington Roebling's Civil War letters to Emily, photographs of the Roebling family and their Trenton estate, and Emily's paper, "A Wife's Disabilities."

Websites
http://roeblingmuseum.org
http://xroads.virginia.edu, American Icon: Incorporating Tension in the Brooklyn Bridge
http://brooklynology.brooklynpubliclibrary.org, Brooklyn Today blog
http://asteria.fivecolleges.edu

CHAPTER 7: JOHN WOLFE AMBROSE: BRINGING IN THE BIGGEST SHIPS

Books and Articles
"Ambrose Channel," *Valentine's Manual of Old New York*, George F. Shrady, circa 1910

Libraries and Archives
National Archives, New York City
Princeton University library archives
New York University library archives
Brooklyn Public Library archives
Brooklyn Eagle Archives
The New York Times Archives
New York Daily Tribune Archives
American Journal of Public Health, American Public Health Association
New York City Department of Parks, Jonathan Kuhn, Director of Antiquities, New York City Department of Records

Websites
www.green-wood.com, Green-Wood Cemetery Historian Blog by Jeff Richman, August 7, 2012
www.OratorioSocietyofNY.org

Author Interviews
2003 transatlantic telephone conversation with Arthur B. Ambrose, London, UK

Chapter 8: Lighthouse Kate Walker

Books and Articles
The Keeper of Lime Rock, Lenore Skomal, Running Press, 2001
"Kate Would Be Proud," Timothy Harrison, *Lighthouse Digest*, March/April 2011
"Robbins Reef Lighthouse," Megan Beck, *Lighthouse Digest*, September/October 2014
"A Working Piece of New York History," Douglas Feiden, *The Wall Street Journal*, November 4, 2015

Libraries and Archives
The New York Times archives
Noble Maritime Collection, "Hold Fast" newsletter, various issues

Websites
www.Smithsonianmag.com, "The Lonely, Lifesaving Job of Lighthouse Keepers Revealed at the National Lighthouse Museum," Michele Lent Hirsch, August 7, 2015
www.lighthousefriends.com
www.lighthousemuseum.org, Kate Walker's Story, National Lighthouse Museum
www.njlhs.org
www.nps.gov, National Park Service
www.uscg.mil, US Coast Guard

Author Interviews
Nick Dowen, Nobel Maritime Collection, Staten Island
Barbara Pezzengrilli, great-great-granddaughter of Kate Walker, Staten Island

Chapter 9: Irving Bush's Folly

Books and Articles
Working with the World, Irving T. Bush, Doubleday, 1928
Ocean Racing: The Great Blue-Water Yacht Races, Alfred F. Loomis, William Morrow and Company, 1936
"The Emergence of Cinema: The American Screen to 1907," *A History of the American Cinema*, Charles Musser, Charles Scribner's Sons, 1994
"A Business Man's View of Religion," Irving T. Bush, *The Outlook*, August 31, 1927
Life magazine, September 30, 1940, advertisement

Libraries and Archives
The New York Times archives
Brooklyn Eagle archives

Brooklyn Public Library archives
Archives, the Hill School, Pottstown, PA
Brooklyn Life newspaper, Brooklyn Public Library
"Bulletin of the Merchants Association of Greater New York," April 6, 1914

Websites
www.bklynarmyterminal.com, Brooklyn Army Terminal Website
www.bushterminal.com
www.IndustryCity.com
www.londonist.com, Bush House: A London Landmark Restored, October 2014
www.brownstoner.com, the Bushes and Brooklyn Industry blog
http://members.trainweb.com
http://edblogs.columbia.edu, the Wendell Bush Collection
www.mbenjaminkatzfinebooksraremanuscripts.com

CHAPTER 10: MALCOM McLEAN

Books and Articles
The Box: How the Shipping Container Made the World Smaller and the World Economy Bigger, Marc Levinson, Princeton University Press, 2006
Box Boats: How Container Ships Changed the World, Brian Cudahy, Fordham University Press, 2006
"The Containership Revolution," Brian Cudahy, *TR Magazine*, September–October 2006
"McLean: a Retrospective," Robert Mottley, *American Shipper* magazine, April 2006
"The Passing of a Pioneer," *Drivers* magazine, September 2003
"Malcom McLean," *The Economist*, May 31, 2001

Libraries and Archives
"PortViews," newsletter of The Port Authority of New York and New Jersey, March–April 2006
The New York Times archives
Washington Post archives

Websites
www.inc.com, "Malcolm Gladwell on What Really Makes People Disruptive"
www.AmericanHeritage.com, "The Box That Changed the World, 51 Years Ago Today," April 27, 2007
www.pbs.org, *Who Made America*, PBS series on innovators
www.panynj.gov, Port Authority of New York and New Jersey

CHAPTER 11: ADMIRAL RICHARD BENNIS, CAPTAIN OF THE PORT 9/11

Books and Articles
Rogue Wave: The U.S. Coast Guard on and after 9/11, Chief Petty Officer P.J. Capelotti,
   PhD, USCG Historian's Office, December 28, 2001
"Attack on America: September 11, 2001," interview with Rear Admiral Richard E.
   Bennis, US Coast Guard Oral History Program, May 31, 2002

Libraries and Archives
The New York Times archives
New York Daily News archives

Websites
www.arlingtoncemetery.net/rebennis.htm, Arlington National Cemetery
www.youtube.com/watch?v=MDOrzF7B2g, "Boat Lift: An Untold Tale of 9/11 Resilience," narrated by Tom Hanks

Author Interview
Telephone interview and e-mails with Gloria Bennis

Index

About the Author

Marian Betancourt has published more than a dozen nonfiction books, a novel, and scores of articles on the history of New York and other subjects. She has always lived near New York harbor.